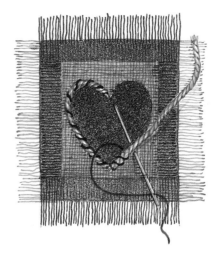

appliqué

appliqué

Lucinda Ganderton

Photography by Pia Tryde

Clarkson Potter/Publishers
New York

pages 1 and 5: Herb Bags (see page 82)
page 2: Floral Tablecloth (see page 74)
page 3: Broderie Perse Throw (see page 66)

Illustrations • Kate Simunek
Pattern & motif drawings • Keith Jackson

Text, design and layout copyright © 1996 Quadrille Publishing Limited
Project photography copyright © 1996 Pia Tryde
Detail photography copyright © 1996 Dave King, Karl Warner

Published by Clarkson N. Potter/Publishers, 201 East 50th Street, New York, NY 10022. Member of the Crown Publishing Group.

Random House, Inc. New York, Toronto, London, Sydney, Auckland
http://www.randomhouse.com

CLARKSON N. POTTER, POTTER, and colophon are trademarks of Clarkson N. Potter, Inc.

Originally published in Great Britain by Quadrille Publishing Limited in 1996.

Manufactured in Spain.

Library of Congress Cataloging-in-Publication data is available upon request.

ISBN 0-517-88718-5

10 9 8 7 6 5 4 3 2 1

First American Edition

contents

Introduction

Appliqué can be defined simply as the process of stitching a small piece of cloth to a contrasting larger one. At a time when woven fabrics were scarce, the unworn parts of a garment would be salvaged and used to repair clothing or furnishings. It was a logical progression for the applied fabric to be cut out in interesting shapes to form a new design, and then stitched down in a decorative manner. From its early utilitarian origins – examples have been found even in ancient Egyptian tombs – the basic process of patching has become a highly versatile needlecraft.

There is a vast international heritage of appliqué, providing an exciting source of inspiration upon which we can build today. Many different cultures have evolved their own ways of working, often utilizing locally available materials in addition to woven fabrics. Native Americans collected dried leaves, beetle wings, and porcupine quills to decorate leather shapes; the Inuits of Alaska used fish skin and feathers; and the bold, bright processional canopies made in India were adorned with dazzling fragments of *shisha* mirror to reflect the sunlight. Tibetan costume and temple hangings, along with *mola* cloths from San Blas in Central America, feature intricate "reverse appliqué," which involves cutting into layers of fabric rather than adding to them.

American appliqué, which is inextricably linked with patchwork and quilting, is still the best-known and most widely practiced method. Applied motifs are often incorporated with patchwork to bring a softer, more flowing element to the designs. Stylized designs of flowers, foliage, cornucopias, and shells – with evocative names, such as Meadow Lily, Princess Feather, Seek No Further, and Horn of Plenty – became a showcase for needlework skills.

There is a certain satisfaction and sense of continuity in recreating an old pattern, and interest in textile history is widespread. However, needleworkers have always been innovative. This book is intended both as a guide to traditional hand-sewn appliqué and as an introduction to newer methods. The projects range from those suitable for a complete beginner to more complex designs for the experienced worker. Drawing on a wealth of traditions, they incorporate a wide range of imagery, fabrics, textures, and embroidery stitches, to convey an overall impression that is unmistakably contemporary.

Getting started

Traditional hand-sewn appliqué techniques have been used by successive generations of needleworkers and quiltmakers worldwide to create a vast array of formal and informal, naturalistic and geometric designs. The traditional turned-under edge method has a bold and direct quality which produces sharply defined shapes, and it can be used for an infinite range of patterns, from simple squares to intricate floral or pictorial motifs.

Only the most basic of sewing skills are required to secure one piece of cloth to another, but today there are new ways of doing this. Comparatively recent developments in bonding fabrics, and the imaginative use of the domestic sewing machine, have both speeded up the process and opened up new ways of working. This chapter introduces the simple tools and equipment needed, and then explores the long-established techniques of turned-under edge and pattern-cut appliqué, along with contemporary methods of machine-stitched appliqué.

materials & equipment

Like its allied needlecrafts of patchwork and quilting, hand-sewn appliqué does not require any expensive or specialized tools. All you need to get started is a basic sewing kit of needles and pins, scissors, a tape measure, and a selection of threads. You will be investing a great deal of time and care in your work, so it is always worth selecting the best-quality tools and materials in order to achieve a lasting and professional result.

Sewing machines are becoming increasingly sophisticated, and many new models are electronically controlled. However, a well-maintained ordinary swing-needle model is all that is required for most machine-stitched appliqué projects.

Sewing tools

All your needlework equipment should be stored for safekeeping in one container. This can range from a workbox with separate compartments for each item, to a simple wicker basket lined with cotton fabric. A traditional housewife, or sewing roll, is still a useful way of keeping essential small items easily accessible, and instructions for making a felt appliqué version are given on pages 50–2.

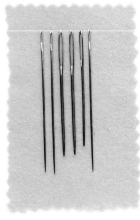

Needles

Needles for hand sewing – each with its own particular purpose – are available in a range of sizes. The thickness of the needle should always be matched to the weight of fabric that you are working with. It is a good idea to buy a packet of needles in mixed sizes to begin with and transfer them to a needlecase for safekeeping. The shiny, plated finish wears off with use, and you should discard tarnished or blunted needles.

• Medium-length "sharps" are used for general hand sewing on most types of fabric and are useful for basting and stitching down appliqué shapes.

• The shorter "betweens" (quilting needles) are good for working slipstitch, as their small size helps to keep the stitches regular and neat.

• Crewel needles are used primarily for embroidery. They have an extra-long eye through which thicker threads can pass without becoming snagged.

Pins

Dressmaker's pins are essential for holding pieces of fabric together before basting and for keeping motifs in place before they are sewn down. A well-stuffed pincushion is the best way of keeping your pins conveniently and safely at hand.

• Special brass lacemaking pins are slightly longer and finer than standard pins and are less likely to leave marks in the fabric.

• Glass-headed pins are helpful when working on large areas or on thick fabrics, as they are easily visible.

Thimble

Thimbles are a practical way to protect your fingers when sewing for a long stretch of time. They are available in wood, metal, or plastic, and should fit snugly but not too tightly.

Scissors

Scissors are important tools, and the blades should always be sharp. It is useful to have four different pairs, each kept for its particular use:

- Medium-sized sewing scissors, which are easier to handle than large dressmaking shears, for cutting out background and appliqué fabrics.
- Small embroidery scissors with narrow, sharply pointed blades, for trimming and notching seam allowances and for clipping off thread ends.
- Paper scissors, for cutting out templates and basting papers.
- Pinking shears, to give a decorative edge to a cutout shape.

Drawing and transferring equipment

You will need a small supply of basic art materials for making templates and planning appliqué designs. In addition, you will need some specialized dressmaker's equipment for transferring your designs onto fabric, all of which is readily available at needlework or craft stores.

Drawing equipment

Basic drawing equipment should include:
- Tracing paper, thin cardboard, and thick paper.
- Clear plastic ruler and draftsman's triangle.
- Pencils and eraser.
- Pair of compasses, for drawing accurate curves and circles.
- Long ruler, for measuring and for marking fabric.

Transferring designs

Designs can be transferred onto fabric in a number of ways.
- Dressmaker's carbon paper can be used to trace a template or an entire design directly onto fabric and is available in both light and dark colors.
- Dressmaker's pens produce an ink line that will fade completely in time, or that is water soluble. This makes them ideal for marking around templates or for drawing freehand on fabric.
- Transfer pencils and pens can be used to trace or draw an outline onto tracing paper or thin paper. This outline is then transferred onto the fabric by dry pressing or simply by applying pressure, depending on the type of marker.
- Using chalk marking pencils or tailor's chalk are more traditional ways of marking shapes, and chalk makes a line that can be brushed away easily.

Fabrics and trimmings

It is, of course, possible to sew any two types of fabric together, but for the most durable results you should choose materials of similar weights, such as finely woven natural cottons, shirtings, and dress prints. Avoid thick fabrics or those that stretch or fray easily. Printed textiles, translucent fabrics, and fancy trimmings can also be effective for appliqué; try experimenting with unusual combinations, as seemingly unrelated fabrics can often work together to provide an unexpectedly dramatic result.

• Background fabrics for appliqué should always have a firm, close weave and be strong enough to support a lot of stitching, but they can be reinforced with fusible interfacing if necessary. If an item is going to receive a lot of wear or will need to be laundered, all the fabrics should be washed and pressed before cutting out to insure that they will not shrink and are colorfast.

• It is not always necessary to buy expensive fabrics for appliqué. Collect scraps and remnants – the random selection of the ragbag can be inspiring in its mixture of textures, colors, and shapes. Lace, organzas, and ribbons, for example, can be combined with printed furnishing fabrics, velvets, or woven brocades to create decorative effects.

• If you cannot find exactly the right fabric for an appliqué project, it is not difficult to add color and pattern to a length of plain white cotton fabric to create your own personal design, and the results can be very satisfying. There are many special fabric paints available in liquid and tube form, and these can be used to paint areas of plain color, to print simple designs from basic blocks, or to draw striped or geometric designs from which motifs can be cut. The colorful motifs on the Kitchen Curtains on page 46 have been created from fabric painted in this way.

• Individual motifs can be cut out from strongly patterned fabrics, such as bold floral prints or *toiles de Jouy,* and rearranged on a plain background to make a fresh design. The motifs can then be embellished with hand or machine embroidery for further decoration. This technique is known as *broderie perse* (see Broderie Perse Throw on page 66).

Threads

Ordinary sewing thread is used for basting and for stitching motifs onto a background, either by hand or machine. The more ornamental cotton, silk, and wool embroidery threads, which come in various weights and textures, can be used to embellish your appliqué designs.

Sewing threads

Threads are available in various thicknesses, different-sized spools, and many colors. Take time to match the thread as closely as possible to the fabric; choose the deeper shade when sewing dark fabrics onto a light background and vice versa. Use a contrasting thread when basting so that the stitches can be easily removed.

• All-purpose polyester thread is versatile enough for most general use. To prevent the thread from fraying when sewing appliqué shapes by hand, strengthen it by running it over a block of beeswax.

• Specially produced quilting thread is made from a mixture of cotton and polyester and has a glacé finish. It is particularly strong, which makes it ideal for hand stitching thick fabrics.

• Cotton or cotton and polyester-mixed threads are designed for ordinary machine use and dressmaking. Machine embroidery threads will give a lustrous finish to satin stitch, but for a very special effect try using finely spun silk or metallic threads.

Embroidery threads

Select embroidery threads to contrast or coordinate with a design – there is a vast spectrum of colors to choose from. Threads as diverse as silk buttonhole twist, crewel wool, and soft embroidery cotton will all give a different decorative effect, but the weight of the yarn should always be compatile with the fabrics you are using.

• Cotton embroidery floss is the most popular and versatile embroidery thread. Its six, loosely spun threads can be used together for a chunky effect, or they can be separated out – two or three strands are commonly used together for finer stitching on lightweight fabrics.

• Pearl cotton (*coton perlé*) consists of a single, tightly spun thread. It comes in three thicknesses and has an attractive, shiny finish.

• Soft embroidery cotton is a thick thread with a matt finish, ideal for bold, decorative stitching.

• Crewel wool is a fine, matt yarn that can be used very effectively for decorating wool fabrics and felt.

hand-sewn appliqué

Turned-under edge appliqué could not be more straightforward, and the technique is quick to master. The design is simply drawn on a piece of fabric and cut out; the raw edge is finished, and the prepared appliqué is sewn onto a background fabric. Closely woven fabrics, such as cotton lawn, are the best choice to start with; they do not fray quickly and are easy to handle. Get the feel for appliqué by starting off with simple straight-edged shapes; then, with practice, you will be able to make elaborate patterns.

Making the templates

Appliqué patterns are usually drawn to their exact size without any additional seam allowance so that they can be traced and transferred accurately onto fabric. The seam allowance is then added on. The patterns for most of the designs in this book are provided in a reduced scale and will have to be enlarged to the required size before they are traced. This is easily done using a photocopier – the instructions for the project will specify the enlargement required.

For a single appliqué motif that will be used only once, a paper shape can be cut out directly from the photocopy or the tracing. If the motif is to be used more than once, the outline should be transferred onto thin cardboard to make a more lasting template. When working with complex, multi-layered designs, trace the individual elements, making a separate template for each shape and labelling each element carefully to avoid confusion later.

Transferring the designs

fig 1

1 Place the template on the right side of the fabric, and line it up along the grain. It is important to match the grain of the cutout shape to that of the background fabric whenever possible, especially when cutting out larger shapes. This prevents the two layers from pulling in different directions and puckering.
2 Secure a paper template by pinning through the center rather than around the outside edge, to prevent the fabric from distorting. Hold a cardboard template in place with one hand. Mark around the template with a sharp chalk marking pencil or dressmaker's fading pen, keeping the line close to the edge of the template.
3 Mark the seam allowance by drawing a second outline ¼" (6mm) outside the first outline (fig 1). Remove the template, and cut out the motif along the outside line. If you are using a non-woven fabric, such as felt or suede, there is no need to add any extra seam allowance, while a fabric that frays easily will need a slightly wider turning.

Preparing the shapes

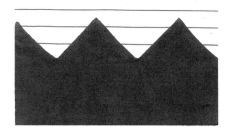

Once the appliqué pieces have been cut out, the raw edges will need to be finished by turning them to the wrong side, basting them in place, and pressing lightly. The basting stitches are removed once the piece has been sewn securely to its background; make sure that all knots in the basting thread lie on top of the fabric so that they can be removed easily. For straight-sided shapes, the seam allowance can simply be folded under without further preparation; curves and angles on a shape are a bit more complicated to deal with as the seam allowance will pucker up or pull if it is not prepared properly before being turned under.

Peaks and valleys

Sharp corners and inside angles are often found on floral or geometric shapes. For a precise outline, the turned-under seam allowance around these appliqué pieces has to be either clipped back or opened out so that the shape will lie flat.

fig 2

Mitering peaks

1 Trim off the outside point, then cut back the extra fabric for a short distance on each side to within ⅛" (3mm) of the outline (fig 2).

2 Fold the point to the wrong side as far as the marked line, then turn under the seam allowance on the two adjacent sides, and baste in place (fig 3). Secure the peak with a few overcast stitches when you are sewing it to the background fabric (see page 17).

Turning valleys

1 For an inside corner, or "valley," clip into the seam allowance to the inside point of the angle, right up to the marked line (fig 4).

2 Turn under the seam allowance on each side of the cut, and baste (fig 5). To prevent the angle from fraying, reinforce it with a few overcast stitches when you are sewing it to the background fabric (see page 17).

fig 3

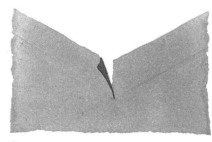

fig 4

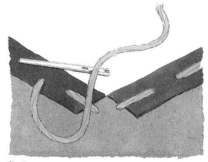

fig 5

Curves

The seam allowance along shallow curves can simply be gently gathered under, but where the curve is tight it will need to be clipped before being turned under, using small, sharp scissors. The tighter the curve, the closer together the cuts should be.

1 Clip into inside (concave) curved edges at right angles, up to ⅛" (3mm) from the marked outline. For outside (convex) curves, remove the excess fabric by cutting out evenly spaced small notches up to ⅛" (3mm) from the outline (fig 6).

2 Turn the seam allowance to the wrong side, and baste in place (fig 7).

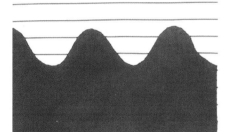

fig 6

fig 7

15

Basting over papers

fig 1

fig 2

When working on a small scale, it is not always easy to clip and stitch the seam allowances neatly on circles or multi-petalled flowers. An effective way of dealing with this problem is to turn the raw edges of the fabric motifs over cutout paper or cardboard shapes that exactly match the templates.

Circles

1 Cut out a disk of thin cardboard to the exact size required. From fabric, cut out a circle ½" (12mm) larger in diameter than the disk, and run a line of closely spaced gathering stitches around the edge. Place the cardboard centrally on the wrong side of the fabric.

2 Pull the thread ends to gather the edge so that the fabric encloses the disk. Arrange the gathers so that they lie evenly and give a smooth outline (fig 1). Press on the right side, then remove the disk carefully.

Flowers

1 First draw around the flower template onto thick paper, and cut out the motif. Then cut out the fabric shape as usual, allowing for a ¼" (6mm) seam allowance all around, and pin the paper shape centrally to the wrong side.

2 Turn under the seam allowance, clipping where necessary, and baste it in place through the paper, making sure that there are no creases (fig 2). Press the shape on the right side using a pressing cloth, then remove the basting thread and take out the paper.

Making bias strips

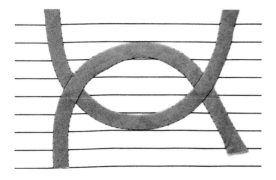

Many appliqué designs feature narrow bands or stripes, such as flower stalks. When these are straight, the fabric is cut along the grain, but curved lines should be cut on the bias, at 45° to the grain. Cutting on the bias makes a flexible strip that will lie flat without puckering. Strips that are less than ¼" (6mm) wide are difficult to handle as the edges tend to fray, so tube-like "rouleau" strips are often used for these.

Turned-under edge strips

1 Cut a paper template that measures ½" (12mm) wider than the finished strip. Pin this diagonally across the fabric, and cut out the fabric strip (fig 3).

2 Press under ¼" (6mm) seam allowances along each side of the strip. Baste the seam allowances down and press lightly, then sew in place.

Rouleau strips

1 Cut out a strip of fabric to twice the required width, plus ½" (12mm). With

right sides together, fold the strip in half lengthwise, and stitch by hand or machine ¼" (6mm) from the raw edge. Trim back the seam allowance to ⅛" (3mm) (fig 4).

2 To turn right side out, first thread a large tapestry needle with a length of strong thread, and secure the thread to one open end of the strip. Pass the needle right through the fabric tube, pulling the rouleau right side out (fig 5). Press so that the seam lies at the back of the rouleau strip.

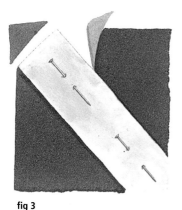

fig 3

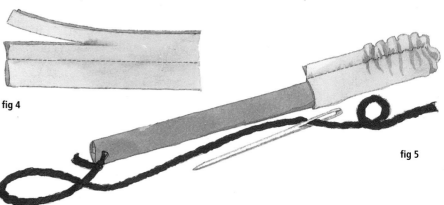

fig 4

fig 5

Assembling the design

Once the various elements of an appliqué design have been prepared, they are ready to be sewn to the background fabric. Most straightforward shapes can simply be positioned by eye, referring back to the original pattern, but geometric or symmetrical designs need to be planned so that the pieces are positioned accurately and overlapping shapes are stitched down in the correct order. For a complex design, dressmaker's carbon paper or a transfer pencil can be used to trace the entire outline onto the background as a guide for placing the pieces.

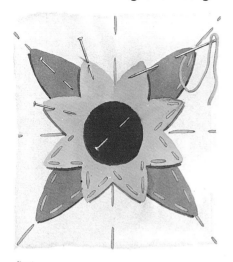

fig 6

Symmetrical designs

Work these logically, pinning down the bottom layers of a multi-layered design first, then placing the smaller and more detailed pieces on top.

1 Fold the background fabric in quarters horizontally, vertically, and diagonally, and press lightly. Mark the creases with contrasting basting stitches. Fold the paper design tracing in the same way so that the two sets of guidelines can be matched.

2 Pin, then baste the individual shapes in place (fig 6), using a ruler as a guide if necessary. Always insert the pins at right angles to the edge so that the pieces lie flat and any wrinkles or puckers can be smoothed out as you work.

Tension

To insure a really smooth finish, small areas of appliqué can be stitched in an embroidery hoop and larger pieces mounted in a square frame. This maintains an even tension across the background and prevents the shapes from puckering. However, it is not essential: if you work on a flat surface and pin and baste each shape carefully, there is no real need to use a frame.

Stitching the motifs

Appliqué shapes can be sewn on in several ways, depending on the desired finished effect. Running stitch is the most basic way of joining any two pieces of fabric and, along with overcast stitch (whipstitch), can be used for non-fray fabrics. Slipstitch is the traditional method of securing turned-under edge appliqué. All three methods can be embellished further with embroidery stitches (see Decorative Stitching, page 36).

fig 7

fig 8

fig 9

Running stitch is used when the line of stitching is intended to show and can be worked in a contrasting color if required. The length of the individual stitches can be varied according to the scale of the work, but they must all be equal and evenly spaced (fig 7).

Slipstitch gives an almost invisible join. Make small, neat stitches, no more than ¼ " (6mm) apart, being careful not to pull the thread too tightly. Bring the needle up just inside the motif, then back over the folded edge and through the background fabric (fig 8).

Overcast stitch (whipstitch) is often used for shapes without a seam allowance. The thread overlaps the edge of the motif and prevents it from fraying (fig 9). A few overcast stitches are used to reinforce the turning of a valley or secure the tip of a peak (see page 15).

Finishing off

Careful pressing, preferably with a steam iron, will give a crisp, professional finish to your work. When all the shapes have been sewn in place, remove the basting threads. Place the finished piece on a padded surface, and press on the wrong side using a pressing cloth.

17

denim banners

This easy project uses the simplest methods of hand sewing to dramatic effect and incorporates the thrifty ingenuity that lay behind much of the earliest appliqué. The faded indigo tones of old, well-washed denim are combined with plain stripes and small-scale prints, some of which were salvaged from an irreparably damaged antique quilt.

The simple shapes, highlighted with contrasting stitching, are reminiscent of both national flags and nautical signals. Rather than being finished, the edges of the flags have been left raw to become a decorative feature in themselves. Pinking shears have been used to give a zigzag finish to the applied shapes.

You will need
Old denim jeans
Old or new striped and printed cotton
  fabric scraps in red, white, and blue
Contrasting cotton embroidery floss
Crewel (embroidery) needle
Pinking shears

fig 1

To make the banners

1 Press the jeans, then check over the lower part of the legs to find areas that show interesting signs of wear. Using a ruler and a draftsman's triangle, mark 3 rectangles, each 8" x 6¾" (20 x 17cm), on the denim. Make sure that each incorporates part of the leg seam, 1½" (3.5cm) from one short edge. Cut out the rectangles following the grain of the fabric, then pull out a few threads along each side to make a shallow fringe.

2 Cut out 3 rectangles, each 3" x 4½" (7 x 11cm), from different striped fabrics, with the stripes running parallel to the long sides. Cut carefully along the grain of the fabric. Again, pull out a few threads along each side to make a shallow frayed edge.

3 Baste the striped rectangles to the denim ones so that one short edge lies centrally along the seam. Thread a crewel (embroidery) needle with two strands of contrasting embroidery floss, and stitch down the rectangles, working small, regular running stitches about ¼" (6mm) from the frayed edge of the striped fabric. The stitches and spaces in between them should not be more than ⅛" (3mm) long.

4 Choose 4 contrasting printed fabrics for the appliqué shapes. Using pinking shears, cut out rectangles 2" x 1½" (5 x 3.5cm), or 1⅝" (4cm) squares. Baste, then stitch them in place with running stitch, again using a contrasting embroidery floss (fig 1). Press the finished piece on the wrong side.

baltimore bride pillow

This American folk-art style pillow is adapted from a single block of a lavish wedding quilt made in Baltimore in the mid-nineteenth century. The rose design was a favorite appliqué pattern, and there are many realistic and stylized variations to be found. This symmetrical version has a large central flower that is balanced by matching buds and smaller blue flowers. Its fresh, contemporary look is achieved by using bold primary colors on a crisp cotton pinstripe background. The pillow is edged with matching piping, but the finishing touch is at the back, where bright covered buttons are held in place with rouleau buttonhole loops. The ambitious quilter could repeat the motif to make a bedspread. Further traditional floral patterns are provided on pages 98 and 99.

You will need
For a pillow 20" (50cm) square:
1⅜ yd (1.4m) blue-and-white pinstripe shirting, 60" (150cm) wide
21" (54cm) square medium-weight fusible interfacing
Plain medium-weight cotton:
    10" x 19½" (25 x 50cm) red
    10" x 12" (25 x 30cm) blue and green
    4" x 12" (10 x 30cm) yellow
Sewing threads in red, green, blue, yellow, and white
84" (2.1m) medium filler cord
8 self-cover button molds, 1" (2.5cm) diameter
Pillow form to fit cover

To prepare the appliqué
1 Enlarge the pattern on page 22 to 150% on a photocopier. Make the templates by tracing the 8 separate design elements – the large flower and 2 parts of its center, the small flower with its center, the leaf, the stem, and the bud – onto thin cardboard. Draw carefully around these onto thick paper to make the basting papers: 1 large flower with center, 4 small flowers with centers, 16 leaves, 8 stems, and 4 buds.
2 Cut out the appliqué shapes from cotton fabric, using the cardboard templates and adding ¼" (6mm) all around for the seam allowances.
3 Baste the flowers, leaves, and buds over their respective papers, clipping the seam allowances as necessary. Baste the stems to their paper strips, but turn under the long edges only. Then press all the pieces, remove the basting, and take out the papers carefully.

To assemble the design
1 Cut out a 21" (54cm) square of pinstripe shirting for the pillow front, and reinforce it with fusible interfacing. Baste horizontal, vertical, and diagonal guidelines across the square in a contrasting color (see page 17).
2 Referring to fig 1, which illustrates the correct order of assembly, center and pin the large red flower in place. Then pin the stems in place along the guidelines, tucking the lower ends under the edges of the petals.

3 Pin on the leaves, then the buds and the small blue corner flowers. Finally, pin on the flower centers.

4 When all the pieces have been positioned correctly, baste them in place. Start from the center and work out to each corner in turn, removing the pins as you proceed.

5 Hand sew the appliqué with slipstitch, using various colored threads to match each shape. Remove all the basting threads, and press the pillow front lightly on the wrong side.

To make the pillow back

1 Cut 2 rectangles of shirting fabric, 12" x 21" (30 x 54cm) and 14" x 21" (36 x 54cm), with the stripes running parallel to the longer sides, to make the 2 sides of the pillow back. Finish one long edge of the wider piece with a narrow double hem.

2 Following the instructions on page 16, make buttonhole loops from 8 narrow rouleau strips of shirting, each 3¼" (8cm) long, and attach these to one long edge of the narrower pillow back piece. Fold

Just over a quarter of the design is shown here. Enlarge it to 150% on a photocopier, and trace the separate elements on to thin cardboard. Add a ¼" (6mm) seam allowance when cutting out the fabric.

22

the fabric in half widthwise, and mark the center. Pin and baste 4 loops on each side of this point so that the ends of the loops are aligned with the edge of the fabric. Leave gaps of ¾" (2cm) between the loops.

3 Cut out a strip of shirting 4" x 21" (10 x 54cm) to make the facing for the buttonhole loops. Finish one long edge, then pin the facing in place over the buttonhole loops with right sides and raw edges together. Baste, then stitch in place, leaving a seam allowance of ½" (12mm) so that the loops are caught in the seam. Turn the facing to the wrong side, and press.

To finish the pillow

1 From the remaining shirting, cut out bias strips 1½" (4cm) wide, joining them diagonally until they measure 84" (2.1m) long. Cover the filler cord with the bias strips, and pin the covered cord to the pillow front, starting at the bottom edge and matching the raw edges.

2 Assemble the three pieces of the pillow cover with right sides together. Making sure that all the stripes run from top to bottom, pin the side of the pillow back with the buttonhole loops along one edge so that the loops point toward the center. Pin the second side along the opposite edge with the hem facing inward (fig 3).

3 Using the zipper foot, stitch around all 4 sides as close to the piping as possible, leaving a seam allowance of ½" (12mm). Trim the corners, and turn the cover right side out. Press lightly.

4 Cover the buttons with plain cotton fabric, following the manufacturer's instructions. Make 2 in each color, and sew them firmly in place on the back of the pillow so that they line up with the buttonhole loops. Insert the pillow form, and fasten the buttons.

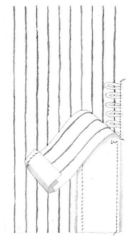

fig 2

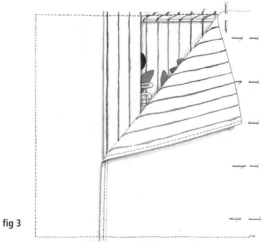

fig 3

machine-stitched appliqué

Provided you are familiar with the controls, using your sewing machine to stitch cutout shapes in place should not prove to be any more complicated than any other sewing or dressmaking technique. Machine stitching gives a distinctive, clear outline to appliqué motifs. It is also quick to do and produces a hardwearing yet decorative finish that is particularly suitable for embellishing garments, quilts, pillows, and any other soft furnishings that will receive a lot of wear or need to be laundered.

Applying the motifs

Motifs for machine-stitched appliqué are cut out to their finished size without any additional seam allowance. This makes the technique ideal for non-woven fabrics, such as felt, which can be attached with a straight stitch.

There can be difficulties when working with fabrics that fray easily. These are usually sewn down with zigzag or satin stitch, and the density of the stitching may become distort the appliqué if it is not basted securely and evenly to the background fabric. Alternatively, special products to prevent raw edges from fraying are available from notions and craft stores. These are painted onto the back of the fabric and are allowed to dry before cutting out.

Fusible web

Joining the appliqué pieces to the background fabric with fusible web solves the problem of the motifs being distorted by machine stitching. The heat-sensitive adhesive web is attached to a paper backing, onto which the motifs are traced. This means that the shapes will not only be accurate but will also be firmly secured to the background across their entire surface so that they neither pucker nor fray as the fabric is stitched in place.

Fusible web is best used for joining lightweight, untextured cottons such as lawn or dressmaking fabrics, and the flat, firm bond that is produced makes it unnecessary to match the grain precisely. Always follow the manufacturer's guidelines on heat settings for the iron, and use a pressing rather than a sliding motion so that the appliqué motif is not pulled out of shape.

1 Trace the outline of the motif onto the paper side of the fusible web, using a sharp pencil, and cut out roughly. Be sure to remember that the cutout shape will be reversed, so if the motif is not symmetrical it will need to be drawn the other way around.

2 With the adhesive side down, place the fusible web on the wrong side of the appliqué fabric, and use a warm, dry iron to fuse it in place (fig 1).

3 Cut accurately around the outline, then peel off the backing paper (fig 2).

4 With the adhesive side down, position the motif on the background fabric. Cover with a damp cloth, and iron it into place (fig 3).

Fabric adhesive

Special fabric glue is useful for fixing in place small appliqué shapes that are to be stitched down by machine or by hand, but it is not suitable for use with fine fabrics. This type of glue is widely available either in liquid form or as a more convenient solid stick.

fig 1

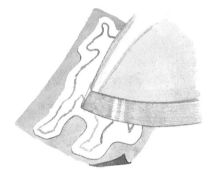

fig 2

fig 3

Stitching the motifs

When stitching motifs by machine, work slowly and carefully, manipulating the fabric as it passes through the machine so that the foot is always parallel to the edge of the motif. Some sewing machines are supplied with a transparent plastic foot which makes it easier to follow the needle. Always make sure that you use a sharp sewing-machine needle; a blunt or damaged point can make the stitching irregular. Match the needle size to the weight of the fabric.

• Standard cotton or polyester sewing thread is suitable for straight or zigzag stitch, but machine embroidery thread produces a more lustrous satin stitch.
• Use the same color thread top and bottom, and try varying the tension; a slightly looser top thread gives a neat edge to a close satin stitch.
• When working on a lightweight background fabric there is a slight tendency for the stitching to pucker, so the work may need to be reinforced with a fusible interfacing.
• An embroidery hoop can also help to maintain an even surface when working on a small area. Mount the fabric so that it lies flat against the machine bed, with the right side facing upward.

Straight stitch

An ordinary machine straight stitch can be used for sewing fabrics that do not fray, as the cut edges do not need to be hidden. Set to a slightly shorter length than for seaming –15 stitches per inch (7 per cm) – to give a more flexible line. Stitch just inside the motif, and keep the needle a steady ⅛" (3mm) from the edge, using the presser foot as a guide.

Satin stitch and zigzag stitch

The zigzag controls on the sewing machine can be set in several ways to produce a stitch that covers the raw edge of a motif. A narrow, open zigzag stitch allows some of the fabric to show through, while a wide, closely set satin stitch is dense enough to hide the edge completely. Whichever version you are using, take time to experiment on fabric scraps, so that you have the best stitch for the particular appliqué you are working on and can handle complicated shapes with confidence.

Points and corners

For outside corners and points, work a line of zigzag stitch to the furthest point, ending with the needle through the fabric on the right. Lift the presser foot, pivot the work around, then continue to stitch along the next side (fig 4). Work inside corners in the same way, pivoting with the needle to the right before continuing along the next side (fig 5).

Curves

To work around a tight outside (convex) curve, pause every few stitches with the needle to the right of the presser foot. Adjust the angle of the fabric so that the foot remains parallel to the edge of the motif (fig 6). When stitching inside (concave) curves, pivot the work with the needle to the left of the foot.

Tapering

A neat, tapered finish can be achieved at both inside and outside corners by varying the stitch width to produce a fine point. This is done by decreasing the stitch width as you approach the corner, pivoting the work, then increasing the width on the second side.

fig 4

fig 5

fig 6

25

hearts edging

The heart is a symbol of romance and devotion throughout the world, and heart shapes were traditionally appliquéd onto marriage or baby quilts to signify affection. This festive border gives a new interpretation to the motif, and the combination of blue chambray, Provençal prints, and gingham ribbon creates a bright, country feel. The heart shapes are edged by machine with a wide band of satin stitch. Alternatively, they could be secured with a decorative hand-embroidery stitch.

The repeat design allows the edging to be adapted to different lengths. A curtain wire runs along the top edge, so that the hearts border can be used to decorate a window, a shelf edge, or a mantelpiece; however, it would also make an attractive window valance or an unusual edging for a window blind.

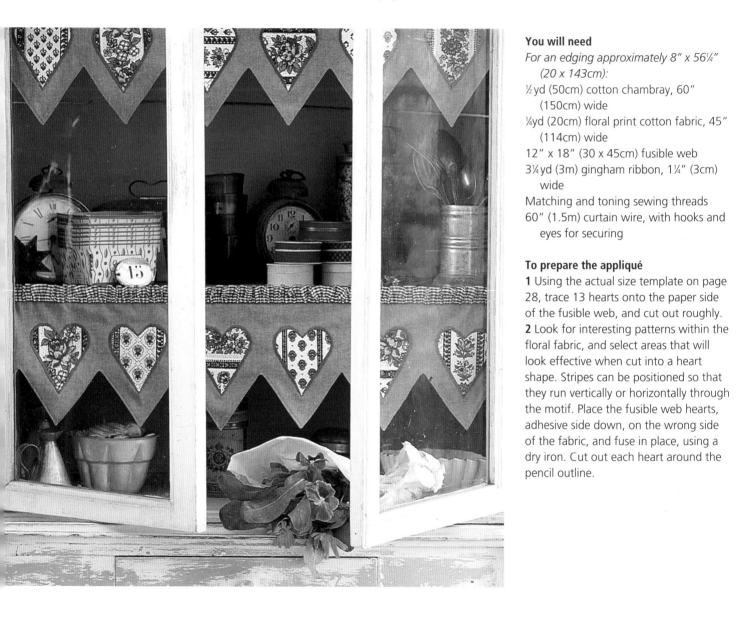

You will need

For an edging approximately 8" x 56¼" (20 x 143cm):

½ yd (50cm) cotton chambray, 60" (150cm) wide
¼ yd (20cm) floral print cotton fabric, 45" (114cm) wide
12" x 18" (30 x 45cm) fusible web
3¼ yd (3m) gingham ribbon, 1¼" (3cm) wide
Matching and toning sewing threads
60" (1.5m) curtain wire, with hooks and eyes for securing

To prepare the appliqué

1 Using the actual size template on page 28, trace 13 hearts onto the paper side of the fusible web, and cut out roughly.
2 Look for interesting patterns within the floral fabric, and select areas that will look effective when cut into a heart shape. Stripes can be positioned so that they run vertically or horizontally through the motif. Place the fusible web hearts, adhesive side down, on the wrong side of the fabric, and fuse in place, using a dry iron. Cut out each heart around the pencil outline.

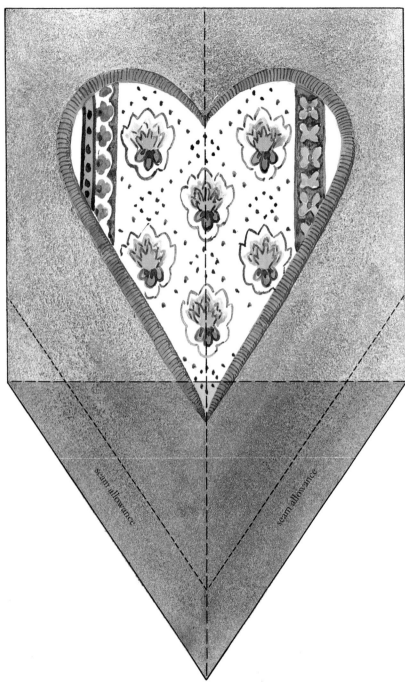

Using the heart shown here as a template, trace 13 heart motifs onto the paper side of bonding web. Use the shaded triangle to mark the zigzag edging.

To prepare the background

1 Using a ruler and a draftsman's triangle, draw 2 long rectangles, each 8³/₄" x 57¹/₄" (22 x 145.5cm), on the cotton chambray, and cut out.

2 Mark the zigzag edging onto the lower long edge of one of the rectangles as follows. Trace the shaded triangle from the template (left), and cut it out. Mark the dividing line. Then mark a line ½" (12mm) in from each side edge of the fabric. Pin the paper triangle to the bottom right-hand corner of the fabric rectangle so that the long side sits on the bottom edge of the fabric and the dividing line of the triangle lies over the marked side line. Using a dressmaker's pen or chalk marking pencil, draw along the diagonal side of the triangle.

3 Unpin and move the paper cutout to the left so that it just touches the previous triangle, then mark the 2 diagonal lines. Continue in this way to the left-hand edge of the fabric (fig 1).

4 With the marked piece on top, pin the 2 fabric rectangles together carefully, placing the pins just inside the zigzag line. Cut out the triangles, and remove the pins (fig 2).

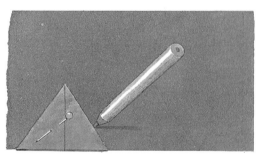

fig 1

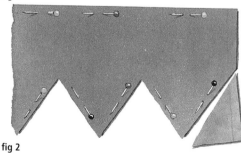

fig 2

To assemble the design

1 Peel the backing paper from the cutout hearts. Using the template on page 28 as a guide, position a heart on each point of one cotton chambray length. Fuse them in place, using a warm iron and a pressing cloth.

2 Thread the sewing machine with toning thread, and set to a close zigzag stitch. (To be sure of a perfect finish, practice on a scrap of fabric first, adjusting the controls until you have a satisfactory satin stitch.) Sew around each of the hearts to cover the raw edges, tapering the stitch at the bottom point of the heart and in the dip at the top (fig 3). Secure the loose ends of thread on the wrong side of the fabric, and press lightly.

To finish the edging

1 With the hearts facing inward, pin the 2 lengths of cotton chambray together, carefully matching the zigzag points and setting the pins at right angles to the edge. Thread the sewing machine with matching thread. With a seam allowance of ½" (12mm), work straight stitch along the two short sides and the zigzag edge.

2 To give a sharp point to the triangles, snip off all the tips and trim back the surplus fabric on each side. At the valleys, clip the seam allowance at right angles almost to the stitching line (fig 4).

3 Turn the edging right side out, and use the tip of your embroidery scissors to ease out each of the points gently. Finish the zigzag edge with a line of machine topstitching ⅛" (3mm) from the seam, and press.

4 Pin the raw edges together, and stitch them with a seam allowance of ½" (12mm). Trim back to ⅛" (3mm). Fold a seam allowance of ½" (12mm) to the wrong side, and press. Fold under a second time, and press again. Pin the double fold in place, and stitch along the lower edge to form a channel for the curtain wire.

5 Finish the two ends of the gingham ribbon, and run a long gathering thread along one side. Pull the end of thread to gather the edge so that the ribbon is the same length as the edging. Pin the ribbon in place over the channel stitching, and stitch down (fig 5). Thread the curtain wire through the channel, and attach a screw eye into each end. Screw the hooks in position as required, and hang up the edging.

fig 3

fig 4

fig 5

pattern-cut appliqué

Pattern-cut appliqué is a striking and deceptively simple technique, and various interpretations have developed in different cultures all over the world. Instead of building up a design from many smaller elements, just two layers of fabric are used, with the applied fabric cut into a decorative pattern before being stitched to the background. The two main variations involve using this top layer to create either a positive or a negative image – in Hawaiian appliqué it is folded and cut into an elaborate motif, while in reverse appliqué areas of fabric are cut away to form the design.

Hawaiian appliqué

fig 1

fig 2

"Album" quilts, consisting of a variety of cut-out "snowflake" patterns on a white cotton background, were made across America in the 1860s, but the technique reached its most elaborate interpretation in Hawaii, where the stylized naturalistic designs were based on the lush local surroundings of waterfalls, vines, and palm trees.

The original Hawaiian quilts were cut from fine percale or sheet fabric that had been dyed in strong colors. Plain white was usually chosen for the background, as this did not detract from the intricate design. Firmly woven cottons are still the best choice for both kinds of pattern-cut appliqué.

Cutting out designs

Instead of cutting the appliqué directly from the fabric, a more accurate result is obtained by making a thin paper template that can then be drawn around. Spend some time experimenting with this method; unexpected and interesting motifs can be created by folding the paper in different ways and cutting out paper "snowflakes" and other attractive patterns.

For example, a simple, symmetrical design, such as a butterfly or tree, can be made by folding just once, while snowflakes and other more complex motifs can be cut from a square piece of paper that has been folded into several segments. A fleur-de-lys motif, created by folding paper in this way, is shown above left.

Remember that over-complicated shapes will prove difficult to handle when transferred onto fabric, and that gently curved and flowing raw edges are easier to finish than sharp angles and geometric shapes.

Assembling the appliqué

1 Cut a square of layout paper to the size of the finished motif. Fold it carefully in half, then in quarters, and then diagonally in eighths. Draw on your design, and cut it out (fig 1).
2 Unfold the pattern, and smooth out the creases (you may need to use a cool iron). Pin the pattern template to the right side of the appliqué fabric, and draw around it, using a dressmaker's pen or chalk marking pencil. Then unpin the paper template.
3 Draw another line about ¼" (6mm) outside the outline for the seam allowance. Cut out the shape around this second line, and clip the corners and curves, using a pair of sharp scissors. Turn under the seam allowance, and baste it in place (fig 2). Press lightly.
4 Mark diagonal guidelines on the background fabric with lines of basting (see page 17). Line up the appliqué shape along these lines, and pin, then baste it in place (fig 4). Sew on using a slipstitch or running stitch.

Reverse appliqué

The design in a multi-layered reverse appliqué is created by cutting away areas of the top fabrics to reveal the colors underneath. The most complex variation of this technique was developed by the people of the San Blas islands off the coast of Panama in Central America. Their *mola* work requires great expertise and can incorporate up to eight or nine different-colored fabrics.

Two-layer reverse appliqué

Equally striking designs can be created from just two pieces of fabric using the method described below. A simple, bold outline should be chosen so that the edges can be turned under and stitched down easily. A quick alternative way of making a more complicated reverse appliqué is to trace the design for the top layer directly onto fusible web. Cut it out carefully – you can experiment with more intricate shapes, as the fusible web will support the fabric – and iron it onto the background fabric. The cut edges can then be concealed with decorative hand embroidery, couching, or machine stitching (see the Decorative Stitching chapter, page 36).

Assembling the appliqué

1 Cut 2 pieces of fabric the same size, and draw the design on the top layer. Remember that this is, in effect, the background color.

2 Baste the pieces together around the outside edge. Working through both layers, stitch a line of basting around the motif outline, about ½" (12mm) outside the drawn line (fig 3).

3 Cutting ¼" (6mm) inside the outline and using sharp embroidery scissors, cut through the top layer, and remove the fabric within the motif (fig 4). Clip the inside angles and curves so that the seam allowance can be turned under.

4 Slipstitch the top layer of fabric to the background along the drawn line. Use the tip of your needle to push under the seam allowance as you work (fig 5).

More complicated appliqué designs, incorporating several colors, can be created following the same method. Cut through one, two, three, or more layers to reveal the underlying fabrics, remembering that the further down the fabrics, the simpler the shapes should be (fig 6). The color that is used least should form the bottom layer.

fig 3

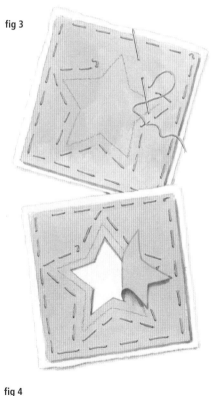

fig 4

fig 5

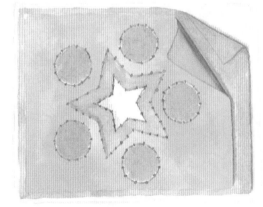

fig 6

snowflake pillows

This unusual trio of small pillows would be ideal for showing off a collection of hatpins, or for displaying brooches on a dressing table. The three variations are made using the same basic method of pattern-cut appliqué. Subtly contrasting shades and textures of pure white cotton, jacquard-weave cotton, and unbleached calico have been chosen to complement the simple, direct designs that are trimmed with looped braid, oversized tassels, and crisp cotton fringe. The pillows could, however, be made in any combination of fabrics. Additional templates are provided on pages 100 and 101.

You will need

For each pillow approximately 6" (15cm) square:
8" x 16" (20 x 40cm) white cotton fabric, to make each pillow form
Polyester toy stuffing
Cream cotton embroidery floss
Matching sewing thread
For the square:
7½" x 24" (19 x 60cm) white cotton fabric
7" (18cm) square unbleached calico

28" (72cm) white cotton fringe, 1" (2.5cm) wide
For the butterfly:
7" (18cm) square white cotton fabric
8" x 21" (20 x 50cm) unbleached calico
4 cotton tassels, 4" (10cm) long
For the circle:
7" (18cm) square white jacquard-weave cotton fabric
7" x 20" (18 x 50cm) unbleached calico
28" (72cm) narrow looped braid edging

Square pillow

To prepare the cutout

1 Enlarge the square motif on page 34 to 130% on a photocopier. Trace the outline, and cut out the template. Cut a 6" (15cm) square from white cotton fabric, pin the template to it, and draw around the outside and inside edges. Add a ⅛" (3mm) seam allowance all around. Clip into the seam allowance around the curves and inside shapes. Finger press the seam allowance to the wrong side, pressing it between your thumb and forefinger.
2 Cut 9 circles 1⅛" (3cm) in diameter from white cotton fabric. Trace a smaller circle ⅝" (1.5cm) in diameter onto thin cardboard. Run a gathering thread around the outside of each circle. Place the cardboard disk in the center and gather the thread tightly. Press on the right side, and remove the cardboard disk carefully (see page 16).

To work the appliqué

Cut out a 7½" (19cm) square from unbleached calico, and place the appliqué shape in the center. Pin, then baste in place. Baste one circle in the center, then arrange 2 on each side. Sew

the shapes on with running stitch, using a single strand of cream embroidery floss. Press lightly on the right side, using a pressing cloth.

To make the pillow cover

1 Pin the white cotton fringe around the edge of the right side of the pillow front so that it faces inward.
2 Cut out 2 rectangles, each 5" x 7½" (12 x 19cm), from white cotton fabric for the pillow back. Fold under and hem one long side of each piece. Place the back pieces face down on each side of the appliqué so that the hemmed edges overlap (fig 1), and pin in position.
3 Machine stitch all the way around the pillow, ½" (12mm) from the raw edges. Trim the surplus fabric from the corners, and turn right side out.

To make the pillow form

Cut out 2 7" (18cm) squares of white cotton fabric, and stitch them together with a seam allowance of ½" (12mm). Leave a small gap on one side, and turn right side out. Fill with polyester toy stuffing, then slipstitch the gap closed. Insert the pillow form into the cover.

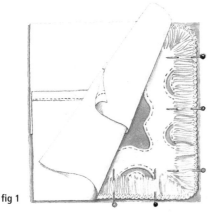

Butterfly pillow

fig 1

To prepare the cutout

1 Enlarge the butterfly motif to 130% on a photocopier. Trace and cut out. Cut out a 7" (18cm) square from white cotton fabric, pin the template to it, and draw around the edges. Add a ⅛" (3mm) seam allowance all around. Cut out, carefully snipping away the fabric within the wing markings.

2 Clip into the seam allowance around the curves and inside shapes so that the appliqué will lie flat, and finger press (see instructions for the Square Pillow).

To work the appliqué

1 Cut out a 8" (20cm) square from unbleached calico, and place the butterfly in the center. Pin, then baste in place. Sew on with running stitch, using a single strand of cream embroidery floss. Press lightly on the right side, using a pressing cloth. Embroider the antennae onto the pillow front with backstitch and French knots, using cream embroidery floss. Then work French knots around the wing markings.

To make the pillow cover

1 Cut out 2 rectangles, each 6" x 8" (15 x 20cm), from unbleached calico for the pillow back. Fold under and hem one long side of each piece. Turn the pillow front face up. Place the back pieces face down on each side of the appliqué so that the hemmed edges overlap, and pin in position.

2 Machine stitch all the way around the pillow, ½" (12mm) from the raw edges. Leave a ¾" (2cm) gap in the stitching at each corner ready for inserting the four tassels (fig 1).

3 Turn the pillow cover right side out. Fold under the raw edges at each of the corner gaps, and push the top of the first tassel into one of these openings. Secure the tassel firmly in position with hand stitching. Repeat to secure the other three tassels.

To make the pillow form

Follow the instructions for the Square Pillow on page 32, using 2 7½" (19cm) squares of white cotton fabric.

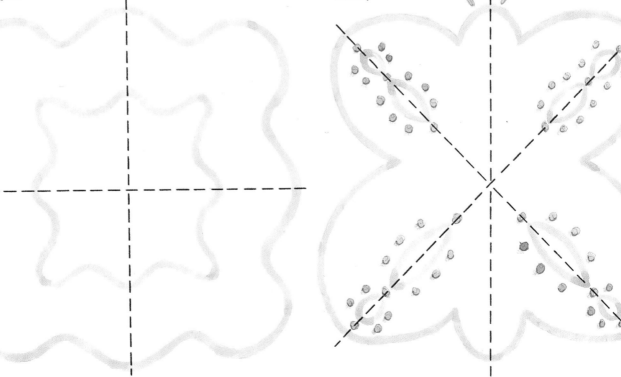

square

butterfly

Enlarge the square, butterfly, and circle motifs to 130% on a photocopier. Add a ⅛" (3mm) seam allowance all around when drawing onto the fabric.

Circle pillow

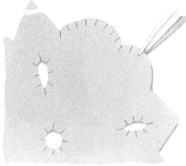

fig 1

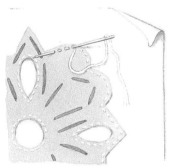

fig 2

fig 3

To prepare the cutout

1 Enlarge the circle motif to 130% on a photocopier. Trace and cut out. Cut out a 6" (15cm) square from unbleached calico, pin the template to it, and draw around the edges. Add a ⅛" (3mm) seam allowance all around. Using sharp embroidery scissors, cut out around the main outline, then carefully snip away the fabric within the central circle and 4 tear-shaped holes.

2 Clip carefully around the seam allowance. Using the ends of the blades, make cuts about ⅛" (3mm) deep into the curves, and trim the corners (fig 1). Clip the central circle and 4 tear-shapes in the same way, and finger press the seam allowance to the wrong side (see instructions for the Square Pillow).

To work the appliqué

Cut out a 7" (18cm) square from white jacquard-weave cotton fabric, and place the cutout in the center. Pin, then baste in place. Sew on with small, neat running stitches, using a single strand of cream embroidery floss (fig 2). Work close to the turned-under edge, pushing

the allowance under with the tip of the needle as necessary. When the stitching is complete, press lightly on the right side, using a pressing cloth.

To make the pillow cover

1 Cut 4 7" (18cm) lengths of looped braid edging. Pin and baste one length of braid along each side so that they face inward (fig 3).

2 Cut out 2 rectangles, each 5" x 7" (12 x 18cm), from unbleached calico for the pillow back. Fold under and hem one long side of each piece. Turn the pillow front face upward. Place the back pieces face down on each side of the appliqué so that the hemmed edges overlap. Pin in position.

3 Machine stitch all the way around the pillow, ½" (12mm) from the raw edges, catching in the looped braid. Trim surplus fabric from the corners, and turn the pillow cover right side out.

To make the pillow form

Follow the instructions for the Square Pillow on page 32, using 2 6¾" (17cm) squares of white cotton fabric.

circle

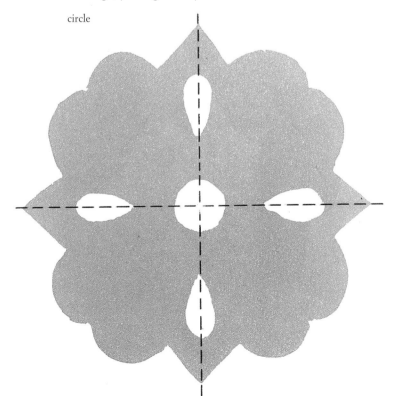

35

Decorative stitching

Hand embroidery has long been combined with appliqué techniques to produce varied textures, colors, and surface decorations. The turned-under edge method of sewing on shapes deliberately uses an invisible slipstitch so that the stitching is unobtrusive. However, when a more elaborate stitch is chosen to secure a motif, the embroidery becomes part of the overall design. The particular threads and stitches selected may complement or contrast with the appliquéd fabrics to either soften or emphasize the outlines. Stitching can also be used to embellish the appliqué shapes, to "draw in" details or to highlight areas of a printed fabric. Machine embroidery stitches can be explored in the same way to add visual interest to appliqué designs, creating a very different effect than hand stitching.

This chapter provides a useful library of decorative hand stitches suitable for appliqué, while the projects illustrate some of the varied uses of both hand and machine embroidery.

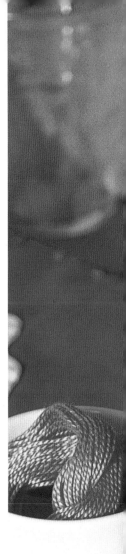

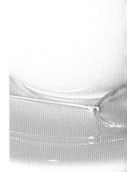

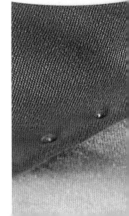

embroidering on appliqué

There is a vast, historic "language" of stitches available to the embroiderer, which can be interpreted to suit any purpose. You may want to create a densely ornamented surface decorated with a range of complex stitches, or, at the other extreme, simply wish to sew around a single motif in a contrasting color. Both are perfectly possible – entire reference books have been devoted to fancy stitchery, and there are many old and new stitch directories available that can prove a fascinating and endless source of inspiration. The stitch library on pages 39–41 describes a range of useful stitches for combining with appliqué techniques. It is divided into outlining, edging, and filling stitches.

Hand embroidery

The addition of embroidered effects using decorative stitches and lustrous threads can be used to enhance a piece of appliqué in a variety of ways:

• To hold down the motifs in place of slipstitch. This can be done using a matching thread for a subtle, textured effect, or with a brightly contrasting color to draw attention to the shape of the motif itself.
• To conceal the edges of a motif by working a line of stitching over the join. This is also a good way to disguise the raw edges of a motif that has been attached to the background fabric with fusible web (see page 24).
• To "draw in" details in a graphic way, either on plain shapes or to emphasize patterned areas within a printed fabric. For example, stitches can be used to indicate the veins on a leaf or even to add spikes to a cactus.

Learning the stitches

Making a traditional sampler is still the best way of learning new embroidery stitches. This will not only produce a useful source for future reference but will also help you get the feel of working evenly and rhythmically. Take time to try out some of the stitches shown in the stitch library on the following three pages. In addition, work out some new variations of your own, and practice

embroidering with different types and shades of thread. Beads, buttons, and sequins can all be incorporated with your stitching.

Starting and finishing

There are not many rules for hand embroidery, but a few points should be kept in mind while stitching to help give your work a professional finish.
• Never work with a thread longer than 18" (45cm). A longer thread will twist and become frayed and worn as it passes through the fabric, giving an untidy look to the stitches.
• Choose a needle that has an eye large enough to be threaded easily and one that will pass through the layers of fabric without being tugged. Too small a needle is also difficult to work with and can damage the thread.
• Most threads can be secured on the wrong side with a tight knot and finished off with a small double stitch worked through the back of the preceding stitches.
• Your stitches should always be of a regular size and equally spaced. Do not pull the thread too tightly or the stitches will become distorted.

Machine embroidery

The decorative qualities of machine stitches should not be ignored. As well as the possibilities for free-motion embroidery, worked with feed teeth lowered or covered, all swing-needle machines have a series of pre-programmed embroidery stitches. With imagination, these can be used to provide a hardwearing and attractive form of decoration for machine-appliquéd motifs.

Outlining stitches

This group of stitches can be used to hold motifs in place on the background fabric, as well as to add ornament. They are usually worked on turned-under edge appliqué to give texture to the plain edge, or on non-fraying fabrics such as felt.

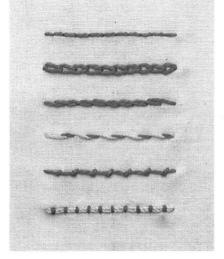

Backstitch
Backstitch is worked from right to left and produces a solid line. Make a row of small stitches, taking the needle back to the end of the previous stitch each time.

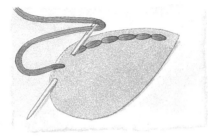

Chain stitch
This makes a flexible, linked line. Loop the thread under the needle as you pull it through. Insert the needle where it last emerged to begin the next chain.

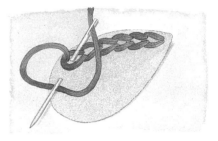

Stem stitch
Also known as crewel stitch, stem stitch is worked from left to right or bottom to top, with the needle always brought up on the left side of the previous stitch.

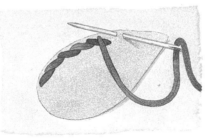

Whipped running stitch
The twisted cord-like appearance of this stitch is created by weaving a second thread under and over a foundation line of running stitch (see page 17).

Coral stitch
This stitch forms an irregular, textured outline. Using the tip of the needle, pick up a few threads at right angles to the stitching line, looping the thread around the needle as shown below.

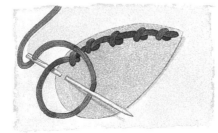

Couching
The technique consists of securing one thread with small stitches of another. Hold the thicker thread around the motif, and catch it down with straight stitches of the thinner thread.

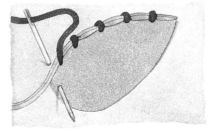

Edging stitches

All the stitches in this group can be worked so that they mask the raw or turned-under edge of an appliquéd motif. If the thread covers the edge completely, there is no need to add an extra seam allowance to the motif.

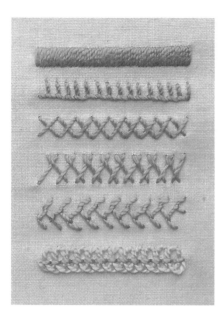

Satin stitch
This stitch has a smooth finish that works well with a shiny thread. The stitches are all worked in the same direction and lie evenly, side by side.

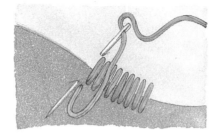

Blanket stitch
Traditionally associated with appliqué, this adaptable stitch is worked from left to right, with the needle always kept at right angles to the edge of the motif.

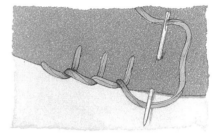

Cross-stitch
Usually worked as a counted-thread stitch, cross-stitch can also be used as an edging on a cutout shape. The top stitches should lie in the same direction.

Herringbone stitch
This stitch forms a wide, decorative band of regular overlapping stitches. Work diagonal stitches in alternative directions, each one separated by a backstitch.

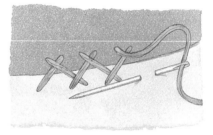

Feather stitch
Feather stitch creates an attractive, open effect, which covers the edges of appliquéd shapes well. Work alternate diagonal stitches, with the thread below the needle to form the loops.

Pekinese stitch
This stitch gives a dense, braid-like border to a motif. Make a foundation row of backstitches, then pass a second thread through this, on the surface only, in a series of overlapping loops.

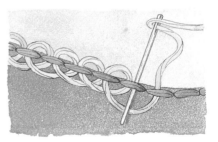

Filling stitches

These detached stitches are used to fill in clearly defined areas, so are ideal for adding texture and color to plain appliqué shapes. Some filing stitches, such as French knots, can be worked singly or in rows.

Fly stitch
For fly stitch, bring the thread through, then make a downward diagonal stitch from right to left, and catch the thread down with a short straight stitch.

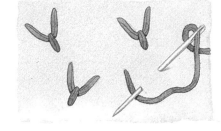

Straight stitch
This simple stitch can either be worked regularly in neat horizontal and vertical rows, or so that the stitches all lie randomly at different angles.

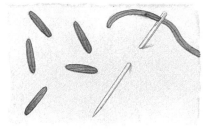

Seed stitch
This little stitch is made by working pairs of short, parallel backstitches that should appear to be scattered haphazardly across the surface of the motif.

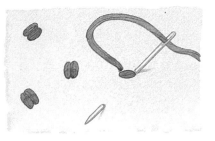

Detached chain stitch
Also called lazy daisy stitch, this variation on chain stitch is constructed in the same way as fly stitch, but with the stitch closed at the top to form a loop.

French knots
Bring the thread through, and keeping it taut with your thumb, twist the needle around it twice. Insert the needle back through the fabric close to the starting point, and draw through to form a knot.

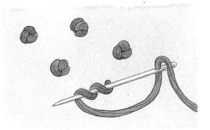

Double cross-stitch
This double stitch is made up of two simple cross-stitches, worked at an angle to each other to create a star shape. The size of the top cross can be varied to form a square- or diamond-shaped stitch.

leaf table linen

Simple stitches worked in bright embroidery threads are combined here with bold leaf shapes cut from vibrant cotton fabrics to give a Matisse-like quality to a striking set of linen that would bring the colors of summer to any table. Make single place mats, or join several pieces together for a coordinating tablecloth or hanging. You may wish to use the templates provided here and on pages 102 and 103, or you could collect your own leaves to make a lasting souvenir of a country walk, perhaps embroidering on the date or the name of the place where you found them for a unique finishing touch.

You will need

For each place mat 12" x 18" (30 x 45cm):

14" x 20" (35 x 50cm) brightly colored heavyweight cotton fabric
8" x 12" (20 x 30cm) contrasting medium-weight cotton fabric
Contrasting colors of cotton embroidery floss, and fine and medium pearl cottons
Selection of leaves (optional)

For the tablecloth 28" x 42" (71 x 107cm):

6 15" (38cm) squares different-colored heavyweight cotton fabrics
6 8" x 12" (20 x 30cm) pieces different-colored lightweight cotton fabrics
Contrasting colors of cotton embroidery floss, and fine and medium pearl cottons
Matching sewing threads
3 yd (2.5m) rickrack

Place mats

fig 1

To make the basic mat

1 Cut out a rectangle 14" x 20" (35 x 50cm) from heavyweight cotton fabric. Turn under a ½" (12mm) double hem around the edge, press with a hot iron, and pin the layers together.
2 Secure the hem with a line of French knots, worked approximately 1" (2–3cm) apart. Use a medium pearl cotton in a bright color so that the stitches will stand out against the background.

To prepare the appliqué

1 Enlarge the templates on pages 44 and 45 to 156% and those on pages 102 and 103 to 136% on a photocopier. Draw around the leaves directly onto contrasting medium-weight cotton fabric. Alternatively, trace around the outline of a real leaf, simplifying any complicated edges. Add a seam allowance of ¼" (6mm) all around, and cut out.
2 Clip up to the drawn line at the points and curve, then fold back and baste down the seam allowance with small, neat stitches (fig 1). Arrange the leaves on the mat, using the templates as a guide if necessary, and pin in place.

To embroider the motifs

1 Using a contrasting fine thread, such as one strand of floss, stitch on the leaves with a regular running stitch (fig 2). Mark the stems using a dressmaker's pen, and sew over the drawn lines with several rows of long backstitches in pearl cotton.
2 Draw the veins on the back of each leaf. Embroider them with straight stitches, using a contrasting fine thread (fig 3). If desired, backstitch the name of the tree in the bottom right corner.

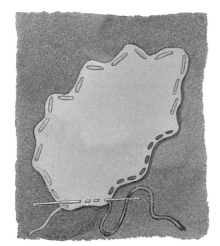

fig 2

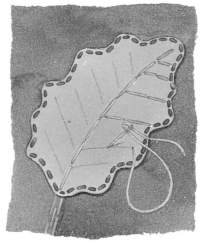

fig 3

Tablecloth

To work the appliqué

Appliqué a different leaf pattern onto each of the squares of heavyweight cotton fabric, following the instructions for the place mat.

To finish the tablecloth

1 Arrange the appliquéd squares in 2 rows of 3 so that the colors balance well. Pin each row together, then sew by hand with slipstitch or by machine using a toning sewing thread, with a seam allowance of ½" (12mm). Press the allowances to one side, then pin the 2 rows together, matching the joins carefully. Press.

2 Stitch rickrack over the seams to conceal the joins, using a matching sewing thread. Turn under a narrow double hem all around, then press and pin in place. Work French knots as for the place mats to keep the hem in place, using a different color of pearl cotton for each of the squares.

ash

oak

Enlarge the leaf motifs to 156% on a photocopier, and use as templates for the appliqué. Add a ¼" (6mm) seam allowance all around when drawing onto the fabric.

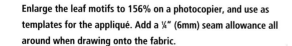

maple

willow

kitchen curtains

The familiar outline of the kitchen teapot forms the centerpiece of these fabric panels. Along with the other tea-table motifs, it is cut from specially painted cotton fabric that does not fray easily. The motifs are sewn in simple backstitch to resemble a drawn line. The stitchery is used both to secure the appliqué to the background and to indicate pattern details, giving a lively, graphic quality to the shapes. This is an adaptable project; the randomly scattered motifs could be arranged to fit any size of panel and painted in colors to match your own color scheme.

You will need

2 lengths checker-textured white fabric to fit your window or cupboard
36" x 20" (90 x 50cm) medium-weight white cotton fabric
Fabric paints in white, blue, yellow, green, red, and orange, or selection of your choice
Paintbrush
Fabric glue
Dark blue cotton embroidery floss
Curtain header tape or curtain wire

To prepare the appliqué

1 Paint pieces of white cotton fabric for the cutout shapes, mixing the fabric paints to achieve the desired shades. Allow at least 10" x 16" (25 x 40cm) in orange; 10" (25cm) square in yellow, blue, cream, and white; 10" x 4" (25 x 10cm) in green, red, and tan. It is a good idea to have extra fabric to work with, and you may wish to experiment with the paint to produce textured, sponged-type patterns. Allow the paint to dry, then press to fix the color, following the manufacturer's instructions.

2 Enlarge the templates shown on pages 48 and 49 to 110% on a photocopier. Cut out the motifs carefully. The cake is made up of 4 separate elements: the cherry, the icing, and the cake and its paper case. Trace individual templates for each of these. Draw separate templates for the leaves, flower, and flower center that decorate the jug.

3 Draw directly around the paper patterns onto the painted fabric, using a soft pencil (fig 1). Cut out the motifs

around this outline, removing the spare fabric within the handles carefully. Reverse the templates for some of the cups so that you have a range of shapes and sizes. To make the panels as shown, you will need to cut out:

orange: 2 sugar bowls, 2 teapots (one facing each way), 2 cups, 1 flower for jug
yellow: 5 candies, 2 cups, 1 flower center
blue: 4 candies, 2 cups
cream: 1 cup, 5 icing tops, 1 spoon, 1 fork
white: 5 cake paper cases, 1 jug
green: 6 candies, 2 leaves
red: 24 cherries
tan: 5 cakes

To assemble the design

1 Fold the lengths of textured fabric in half lengthwise and widthwise to find the center, and place one of the teapots in the middle of each. Lay the pieces side by side on a flat surface, and arrange the other motifs around the teapots to form a balanced layout. You may wish to refer to the photograph as a guide, or prefer to make your own design. When you are satisfied with the arrangement, use a small amount of fabric glue to hold each of the shapes in place.

2 Arrange each cake so that the cake goes down first, with the icing and the cake paper overlapping it at top and bottom. Each cake is topped with a cherry. Secure the flower on the milk jug with one leaf on each side. The yellow circle is glued in the flower center.

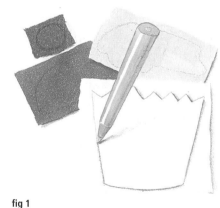

fig 1

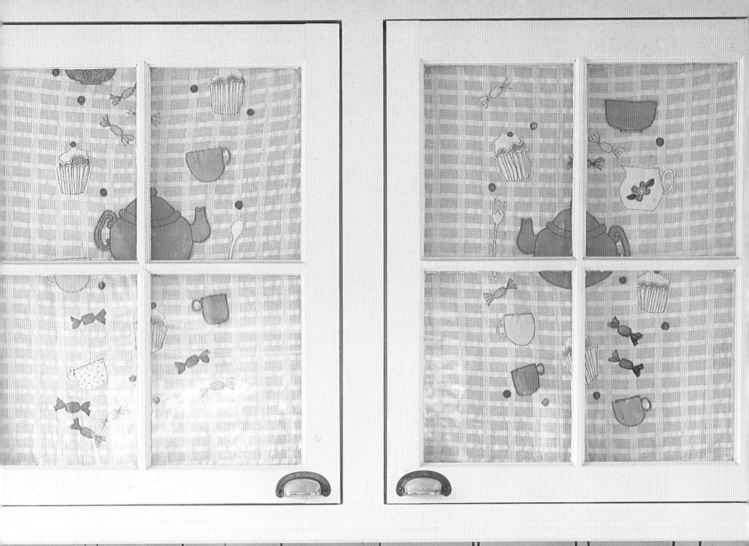

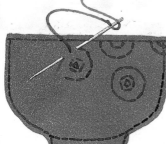

fig 2

fig 3

To embroider the motifs

1 The motifs are all held down with backstitch, which is also used to indicate the details of each motif. Sew with a single thread of dark blue embroidery floss for a fine line. Make the stitches fairly large, and do not worry if they are not perfectly regular – this will give an informal air to the stitchery. Follow the lines on the templates as a guide to where the details need to be filled in.

2 The spotted design on the white teacup is indicated with seed stitch, and the concentric circles on the sugar bowl are worked in backstitch (fig 2). The folds on the cake paper case are worked with long, single straight stitches (fig 3).

To finish the curtains

Make a double hem of ½" (12mm) along each side and the bottom edge of both curtain panels, mitering the corners. They can be finished off with a curtain header tape or a curtain wire threaded through a channel at the top, depending on where they are to hang.

Enlarge the motifs to 110% on a photocopier, and use as templates for the appliqué.

workbag, housewife, & needlebook

A special container for needlework tools and materials is essential for everyone who enjoys sewing. This festive set of matching workbag, needlebook, and old-fashioned "housewife" will insure that your equipment is always stored safely in the same place and can be carried with you wherever you are working.

The needlebook, with its felt "pages," is the best way to keep your needles at hand, as they are liable to get lost inside a pincushion, while a roll-up housewife has long been a favorite method of safeguarding scissors, ruler, tailor's chalk, and other essentials. The roomy base of the workbag is made from felt-covered cardboard trimmed with harlequin diamonds and embroidered circles, in colors chosen to coordinate with the floral print of the drawstring top.

Housewife

You will need

Felt as follows:

    12" x 18" (30 x 45cm) dark blue

    6" x 6" (15 x 15cm) pink

    6" x 3" (15 x 7.5cm) green

    6" x 3" (15 x 7.5cm) white

Matching dark blue, pink, and green embroidery floss

To make the cover

1 From dark blue felt cut 2 main pieces, each 8" x 12" (20 x 30cm). Enlarge the templates for the petals and the flower center on page 53 to 143% using a photocopier. Use these to cut from felt: 6 white, 4 green, and 4 pink outer petals; 7 green and 7 pink inner petals; 1 white and 1 pink flower center.

2 Arrange the outer petals to form 2 flower shapes at the edge of one of the main pieces. Make a 6-petalled white flower and an 8-petalled flower with alternate green and pink petals, overlapping some of them. Pin, then blanket stitch in place, using contrasting pink floss for the white petals and dark blue for the other flower.

3 Pin the inner petals to the flowers, alternating pink with green. Sew in place with straight stitches worked at right angles to the edges of the shapes, using dark blue embroidery floss. Attach the pink flower center to the white flower and the white flower center to the other flower with blanket stitch, using green embroidery floss. Decorate with a few contrasting French knots.

To make the inside

1 Enlarge the patterns for the pockets and pencil holder on page 53 to 143% on a photocopier. Cut out the shorter pocket (1) in green felt, the scissor pocket (2) and the taller pocket (4) in pink felt, and the pencil holder (3) in white felt. Pin these pieces in place on the second main piece.

2 Sew on the pockets with blanket stitch, using a contrasting floss for each felt color. Secure the ends of the pencil holder 2½" (6.5cm) apart with blanket stitch. Sew 3 lines of running stitch to divide it into 4 loops to hold pencils, crochet hooks, or markers (fig 1).

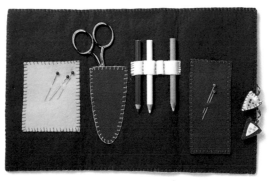

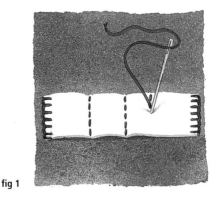

fig 1

fig 2

To make the fastening

1 Cut 3 12" (30cm) lengths from each of the 3 colors of cotton embroidery floss to make the tie cord. Knot tightly at one end, and braid them together. Tie the other end in a knot and trim the loose ends.

2 Enlarge the template outlines on page 53 to 143% on a photocopier, and cut one large and one small triangular tab from each of the 4 different-colored felts. Choosing contrasting colors, secure the inner triangles in place on the larger triangles with 4 French knots.

3 Join 2 of the triangles together along the long sides with blanket stitch, and slip this over one of the knotted ends of the tie cord. Sew the third side together with blanket stitch, securing the tie cord

in place (fig 2). Make the other tab in the same way, and secure it over the other knotted end of the tie cord. Fold the cover into thirds and sew the tie cord in place at its center, halfway along the folded edge.

4 Enlarge the button templates on page 53 to 143% on a photocopier, and cut a large pink and a smaller green circle from felt. Join the circles with a few dark blue French knots, and stitch onto the appliquéd side of the cover in line with the tie.

To finish the housewife

Pin the inside piece to the wrong side of the cover. Join them together around the outer edge with blanket stitch worked in pink stranded cotton.

Needlebook

You will need

Felt as follows:
    6" x 7" (15 x 18cm) dark blue
    6" x 9" (15 x 23cm) green
    6" (15cm) square pink
Matching dark blue, green, and pink
    cotton embroidery floss
Pinking shears

To cut out the pieces

1 Cut out a rectangle of dark blue felt 5" x 7" (12.5 x 18cm) for the main cover. Make the inner pages from one rectangle of pink felt 4" x 6" (10 x 15cm) and one rectangle of green 3½" x 5" (9 x 12.5cm). Cut out the pages, using pinking shears.

2 Enlarge the templates on page 52 to 143% on a photocopier. Trace the zigzag panel and use to cut the motif from green felt. Trace the 2 diamond-shaped petal templates and the circular flower center. Cut 4 pink and 4 dark blue petals from both the large and small templates, and 2 green flower centers.

To make the cover

1 Lay the 8 larger petals in place on the right-hand side of the green zigzag panel. Place them in a flower shape, alternating the pink and blue petals and overlapping them slightly as you go around. Pin, then blanket stitch them in place, using green floss. Stitch as far around each petal as you can.

2 Sew the green flower center to the middle of the flower so that it conceals the ends of the petals. Use blanket stitch, worked in pink floss (fig 1).

3 On the left-hand side of the background piece, work the smaller flower in the same way.

4 Using dark blue embroidery floss, work a sprinkling of evenly spaced French knots across the background, and finish off the flower centers by working 3 knots on each.

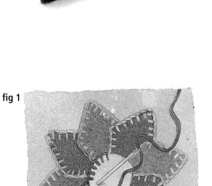

fig 1

fig 2

5 Baste the appliquéd piece in place on the main cover. Sew it all around the outer edge with blanket stitch, using pink embroidery floss. Try not to take the needle right through the blue felt background so that the stitches do not show on the wrong side.

To finish the needlebook

Lay the 2 inner pages inside the main cover of the needlebook, and pin in place. Fold the cover in half to find the exact center line, then using pink embroidery floss, backstitch the 3 layers together along the spine (fig 2).

Needlebook

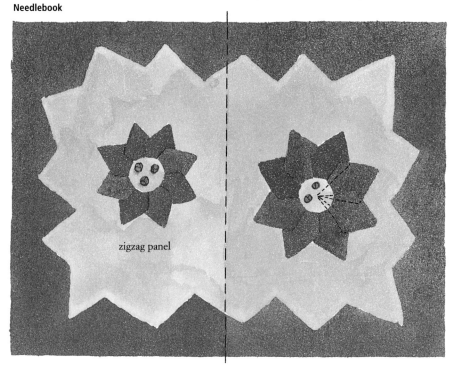

zigzag panel

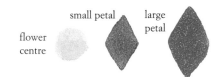

flower centre   small petal   large petal

Enlarge all the templates to 143% on a photocopier.

Housewife

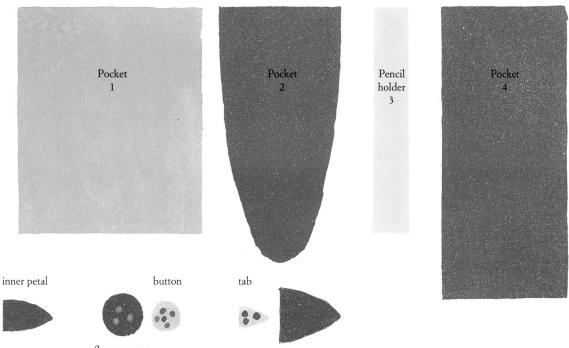

Pocket 1

Pocket 2

Pencil holder 3

Pocket 4

outer petal   inner petal   button   tab

flower center and button

Workbag

outer diamond

inner diamond

outer circle   inner circle

Enlarge the templates to 143 % on a photocopier.

You will need
Felt as follows:
>   16" x 28" (40 x 71cm) dark blue
>   10" (25cm) square green
>   10" (25cm) square pink

Matching dark blue, pink, and green
cotton embroidery floss
10" x 27" (25 x 69cm) cotton fabric with
small-scale floral print
24" x 27" (61 x 69cm) pink cotton
fabric, for lining
Sewing thread to match cotton fabrics
16½" x 23½" (42 x 60cm) sheet medium-
weight cardboard
Masking tape
Fabric glue
Metal ruler
Craft knife
Safety pin

To make the drum
1 Using a draftsman's triangle, draw a
rectangle 6" x 26" (15 x 66cm) on
medium-weight cardboard. Using a pair
of compasses, draw a circle with a radius
of 4½" (11.5cm). This will be the base.
Draw a circle with a radius of 4" (10cm)
inside the main circle. Cut out both
shapes accurately, using a craft knife.
2 Score along the outline of the inner
circle, then snip around the outer edge
to form tabs. Bend these upward. Curve
the rectangle into a cylinder, overlapping
the edges by ½" (12mm). Glue the edges
together, using fabric glue, and tape

down with masking tape. Spread a thin
layer of glue on the outside of the tabs,
and fit the cylinder over the base (fig 1).
Secure with extra tape if necessary.

To cover the drum
1 Cut out a rectangle 6½" x 26½"
(16.5 x 68cm) from dark blue felt. This
rectangle is decorated before being
glued to the drum.
2 Enlarge the 2 circle templates given
below left to 143% on a photocopier.
Cut out from felt 7 green and 7 pink
outer circles, and 7 dark blue, 4 pink,
and 3 green inner circles. Pin them
together in pairs, and arrange along the
rectangle of dark blue felt. Baste, then
stitch in position using contrasting
embroidery floss. Use either blanket
stitch, a scattering of French knots, or
double cross-stitch.
3 Spread a light coat of glue over the
drum, and wrap the appliquéd felt
around it. Fold a ½" (12mm) allowance
over the top edge, and glue down. Allow
an overlap of ½" (12mm) at the side. To
secure the side seam, work a line of
blanket stitch over the cut edge, using
pink embroidery floss. Draw a circle with
a radius of 4" (10cm) on a piece of
paper, cut out and use this as a template
to cut out a circle of dark blue felt. Glue
to the drum base. Using pink embroidery
floss, sew a line of decorative blanket
stitch around the bottom edge (fig 2).

fig 1

fig 2

fig 3

fig 4

To make the gathered top

1 Cut out a circle with a radius of 4½" (11.5cm) from pink cotton fabric, using a paper template as a guide as before. Cut out a rectangle 15" x 27" (38 x 69cm) from the same fabric. With right sides facing, fold the rectangle in half, and sew the 2 short edges of the rectangle together with a seam allowance of ½" (12mm). Press the seam open. With right sides together, pin the circle to the lower edge of this cylinder, and sew around the outside edge.

2 Cut out a rectangle 10" x 27" (25 x 69cm) from floral-print cotton fabric. With right sides facing, join the 2 short edges, leaving a ½" (12mm) seam allowance. Press the seam open, then pin to the open top edge of the lining, right sides together. Then sew the 2 workbag pieces together with a ½" (12mm) seam allowance to form a long duffle-bag shape (fig 3).

3 Turn the floral fabric to the right side, and press the folded seam. Cut out a 26" (66cm) strip of dark blue felt, ¾" (2cm) wide, to form the drawstring channel. Turn under ¼" (6mm) at each short end, and pin the strip around the top edge 1½" (4cm) from the fold. Stitch in place along both long edges with blanket stitch, using green embroidery floss (fig 4).

To finish the workbag

1 Place the fabric top inside the covered drum, and pin the raw edge of the floral fabric to the inside of the rim. Sew firmly in place, stitching through the lining, the floral fabric, and the felt. The diamond trim will conceal this join.

2 Enlarge the inner and outer diamond templates on page 54 to 143% on a photocopier, and cut out from felt 10 pink and 10 green outer diamonds, and 20 dark blue inner diamonds. Join them in pairs with a few French knots, using pink floss. Overcast stitch around the outer edges in a contrasting color – green for the pink diamonds and dark blue for the green.

3 Sew the diamonds around the rim of the workbag, securing them to the felt with a few overcast stitches on either side so that the top and bottom points are left free. Alternate the colors for a harlequin effect.

4 Make the drawstring cord by braiding together three 24" (60cm) strands of each color of embroidery floss. Knot firmly at each end, then fasten one end to a safety pin. Thread this through the drawstring channel.

5 For the decorative tabs that cover the ends of the cord, cut out 2 inner and 2 outer diamonds each in dark blue and again in green felt. Join them together as before with French knots, using pink embroidery floss, then pin in pairs on each side of the cord knots. Join together with blanket stitch worked in pink embroidery floss.

alphabet quilt

This quilt, which could also be used as a nursery hanging or play mat, was inspired by traditional teaching quilts, made to introduce the alphabet to small children in an informal way. The favorite nineteenth-century color scheme of turkey red on white gives the quilt a fresh appeal.

The quilt is practical as well as decorative: the fabrics used – medium-weight cotton, check homespun, and polyester batting – are all washable. The appliqué is finished with machine zigzag, so it will withstand hard wear. The alphabet, numerals, and extra motifs are given on pages 104, 105, 108, and 109.

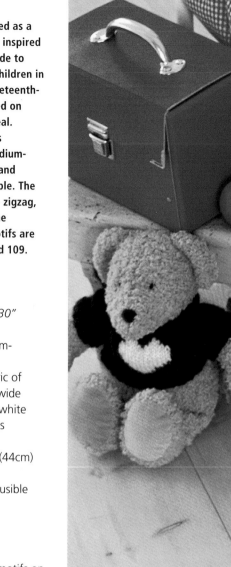

You will need
For a finished quilt (or playmat) 30" *(75cm) square:*

30" (75cm) square white medium-weight cotton fabric

30" (75cm) dark red cotton fabric of similar weight, 45" (115cm) wide

16" x 32" (40 x 80cm) red-and-white checked cotton fabric, such as homespun

11/2yd (1.4m) fusible web, 17" (44cm) wide

30" (75cm) square lightweight fusible polyester batting

Red and white sewing threads

To prepare the motifs
1 Enlarge the templates for the motifs on pages 58 and 59 to 154% and the letters on pages 108 and 109 to the size indicated, using a photocopier. Cut out, and turn face downward. Trace the reversed outlines onto the paper side of the fusible web, leaving at least ½" (12mm) between them. To make the quilt as illustrated, you will need the entire capital and lower-case alphabets, 4 stars, 2 shoes, 2 socks, bucket and shovel, scissors, bird, camel, giraffe, rattle, spoon, and fork.

2 Cut out the letters and motifs roughly. Cut out a 30" (75cm) square from dark red cotton fabric to make the backing, and use the remainder of this fabric for

the motifs. Place the motifs adhesive side down on the fabric, following the grain, and fuse in place using a dry iron. Trim around the outline of each shape.

To prepare the background
1 Cut out a 17½" (45cm) square from paper to act as a template for marking the center panel. Fold it in half vertically, horizontally, and diagonally to find the center. Fold the square of white cotton

fabric in the same way, pressing each fold lightly. Use these creases as a guideline to pin the paper square to the center of the fabric. Mark around the 4 sides of the square, using a chalk marking pencil (fig 1), unpin and remove the paper square.

2 Using a ruler measure a line 1½" (4cm) outside each side of the square, and draw this in as a guide for placing the capital letters (fig 2).

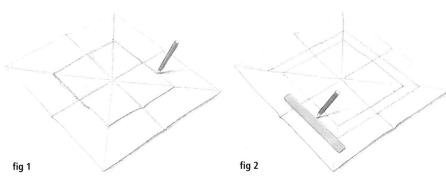

fig 1   fig 2

Placement diagram for the quilt

To position the motifs

1 Sort the capital letters into 4 groups: A–F, G–M, N–T, and U–Z. Arrange one group along each side of the marked square, making sure that the letters are evenly spaced and placed in alphabetical order. Fuse one letter in place at a time, removing its backing paper and pressing it carefully. Fuse a star motif in each of the four corners of the square to complete the border design.

2 The lower-case letters and motifs are scattered within the center panel. You can use the photograph on the left as a guide, or make your own arrangement. Take some time to find a satisfying layout. Insure that the outer shapes all butt against the square outline to define the center panel. Fuse each of the arranged motifs in place in the same way as for the alphabet.

To stitch the motifs

1 Using white sewing thread, work the machine-embroidered details. The automatic patterns vary between machine models, so experiment to find stitches that you like.

The motifs on the quilt illustrated are decorated as follows. The tops of the socks are indicated with 3 parallel bands of stitching. The rattle is decorated with 2 lines across the center, and there are 3 straight-stitch stars on the bucket. A narrow zigzag is used on the spade and for the bird's wing. Its eye, and those of the camel and giraffe, are marked with satin stitch. The inside line on the shoes is also zigzagged, and the sunburst motif and buttons are in satin stitch. Use a needle to pass all the loose ends of thread through to the back of the work, and secure.

2 Thread the machine with red sewing thread, and set the controls to a narrow zigzag. Stitch around the outside of each shape to cover the raw edges. Work slowly and carefully, especially around the curves, and pivot the work at the corners to give a neat outline (see page 25). Secure all the loose ends, and press the quilt top.

To finish the quilt

1 Following the manufacturer's instructions, fuse the batting to the back of the appliquéd square. Baste the dark red fabric backing in place around the four edges.

2 Cut the checked cotton fabric into 4 strips, each 4" x 32" (10 x 80cm), to make the bindings for the edges. Press each strip in half lengthwise, then press under a seam allowance of ½" (12mm) along both sides of each strip. Bind the raw edges with these strips, finishing each corner by trimming and turning under the raw edges of strip, and slipstitching the outside edge.

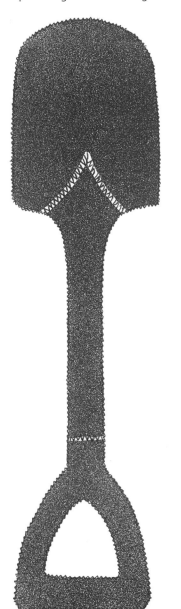

59

Enlarge the motifs to 154% on a photocopier, and use as templates for the appliqué.

animal scarves

Appliqué is very adaptable and can be used easily to decorate a wide range of ready-made items. These standard woolen scarves have been transformed into distinctive and desirable accessories by adding animal motifs cut from felt. The hart and hind (deer) lend a baronial air to traditional tartan, while brightly colored dogs stand out from their purple background.

Craft felt is available in a wide variety of both strong and muted colors. It is made from natural wool fibers, so it works well in conjunction with other woolen fabrics. Because it is not woven, the cutout shapes will not fray, making felt particularly suited to the intricate and detailed shapes used here. Machine stitching in contrasting colors secures the motifs in position while adding a decorative touch.

Hind and hart

You will need
Fringed tartan woolen scarf
Felt as follows:
    8" (20cm) square coral
    5" x 6" (13 x 15cm) olive-green
    Scraps of black, white, and lilac
Red heart-shaped button
80 white shirt buttons, ¼" (7mm)
    diameter
14 interestingly shaped wooden buttons
3 self-cover button molds, 1" (2.5cm)
    diameter
Scraps of red tartan fabric, to cover
    buttons
Red, black, and white sewing threads
Green tweed-effect knitting yarn
Large-eyed needle
Fine-point indelible felt-tip pen

To work the appliqué
1 Enlarge the hind and hart outlines given on page 63 to 156% using a photocopier, and cut out. Trace the heart outline, and make a separate paper template for this.
2 Turn over the pattern for the hart, and pin it to the coral felt. Draw lightly around the outside of the hart and the space between body and legs, using an indelible felt-tip pen. Remove the hart template, and cut out around the ink line, using sharp scissors. Repeat for the hind template, using olive-green felt. Cut out the heart from lilac felt. Felt is difficult to mark, so transferring the outlines in this way means that the line will not show on the right side. Cut out 3 small circles for the eyes from both black and white felt.

3 Pin the hart centrally at one end of the scarf 1½" (4cm) from the fringe so that it is facing toward the right. Baste in place, then machine stitch, using red sewing thread. Use a straight stitch, and keep the stitching line ⅛" (3mm) in from the edge of the felt. Baste the lilac heart onto the hart's body, and machine stitch, using red sewing thread. Sew the hind centrally to the other end of the scarf 4" (10cm) from the fringe, using red sewing thread, and attach a red heart-shaped button to its back. Stitch the eyes for both animals in place by hand, placing the smaller black felt circles over the white felt circles.

To finish the scarf
1 The antlers for both hind and hart are made from tiny shirt buttons. Follow the lines on the template as a guide to placing, and stitch them on using white sewing thread.
2 Stitch 12 wooden buttons randomly around the hart, using tufts of green tweed-effect knitting yarn. Thread a large-eyed needle with a length of yarn, and sew the first button firmly in place. Leave the 2 loose ends at the front, knot securely, and trim. Repeat for the other 11 buttons.
3 Following the manufacturer's instructions, cover 3 self-cover button molds with red tartan fabric. Use these 3 red tartan covered buttons and 2 more wooden buttons to decorate the opposite end of the woolen scarf below the hind, stitching the butons on using tufts of yarn as before.

Dog and tree

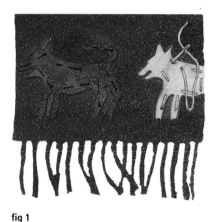

fig 1

You will need

ringed purple woolen scarf
Felt as follows:
   7" x 10" (18 x 25cm) lime-green
   5" x 8" (13 x 20cm) orange
   5" x 8" (13 x 20cm) bright pink
   5" (13cm) square ocher
   Scraps of purple, dark green, and rust
⅜" (10mm) shirt buttons:
   10 blue
   15 red
   3 yellow
Dark orange, red, dark blue, and yellow
   sewing threads
Fine-point indelible felt-tip pen

To work the appliqué

1 Enlarge the tree and dog outlines below and opposite to 156% on a photocopier, and cut out. Reversing the templates as for the Hind and Hart Scarf, draw lightly around the outlines, using an indelible felt-tip pen, and cut out from felt: a lime-green tree shape, an orange right-facing dog, a bright pink left-facing dog, and an ocher left-facing half-dog. Cut 4 purple, 3 lime-green, 3 rust, and 10 dark green leaves.

2 Pin and baste the orange dog and the tree to one end of the scarf, and the bright pink and ocher dogs to the other end, 1½" (4cm) from the fringe (fig 1). Thread your machine with dark orange sewing thread, and sew the dogs in place with straight stitch, ⅛" (3mm) in from the edge of the felt. Stitch the tree in place, using red sewing thread.

3 The dogs are decorated with buttons and felt leaf shapes. The leaf shapes are machine stitched on lengthwise, using yellow sewing thread. For the buttons, use contrasting or matching thread as required. Using the templates and photograph as a guide, stitch 4 purple leaves and 4 blue buttons onto the orange dog, and 3 lime-green leaves and 3 yellow buttons onto the pink dog. Scatter the remaining 6 blue buttons across the ocher dog's body.

4 Machine stitch 10 dark green leaves around the tree and 3 rust-colored leaves at the bottom of the trunk. Using a double length of red sewing thread, stitch the red buttons firmly onto the branches. Leave the ends of the thread at the front, and trim to 1" (2.5cm).

cut here for half-dog

dog for dog and tree scarf

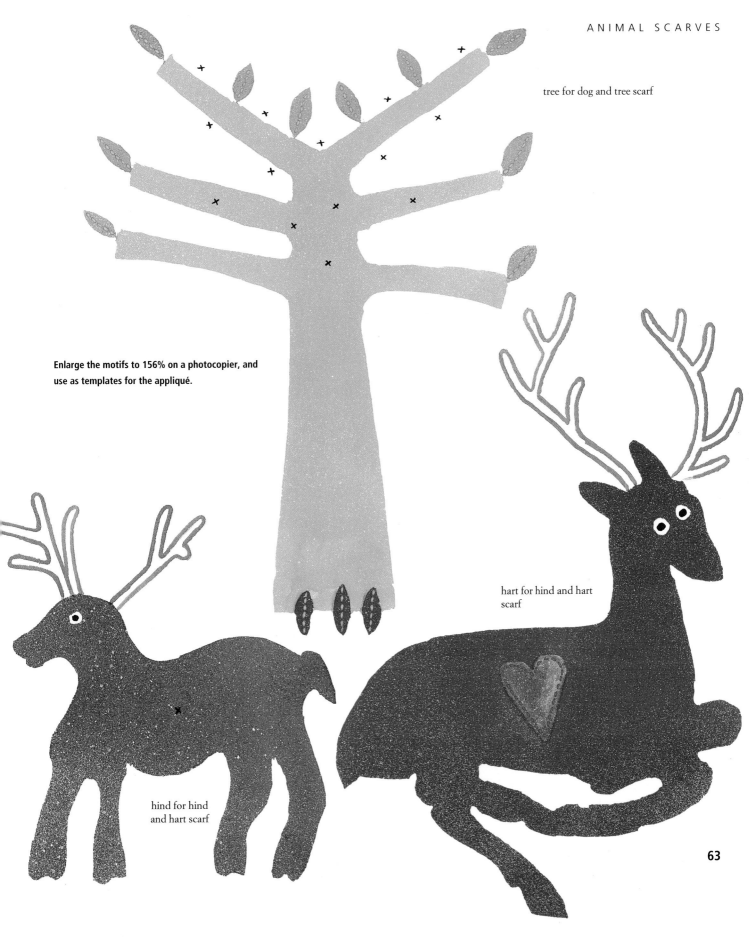

tree for dog and tree scarf

Enlarge the motifs to 156% on a photocopier, and use as templates for the appliqué.

hart for hind and hart scarf

hind for hind and hart scarf

63

Printed & patterned fabrics

Plain cottons and silks have been decorated using various printing techniques for many hundreds of years, to produce a wide array of patterned fabrics for clothing and interiors. The simplest hand-block methods have developed into the sophisticated screen- and roller-printing processes of today, and an array of modern and traditional prints is now available.

Printed fabrics are an ideal source of inspiration for creating new appliqué designs. Individual motifs can be cut out from a patterned fabric; brightly colored patterns can be used together with woven stripes, tweeds, and ginghams to create a variety of new designs. The projects in this chapter show some of the ways in which fabrics can be combined.

broderie perse throw

A varied selection of upholstery remnants and fabric samples in contrasting textures has been gathered together to make this broderie perse throw. The lush floral arrangement blends multicolored motifs cut from glazed chintzes and union cloth with simple leaf shapes from coordinating plain fabrics. The white linen background gives a crispness to the design, which is highlighted by using embroidery stitches both to secure the shapes and add detail. The piece is interlined to give it extra weight and is backed using toning blue cotton fabric with a matching border of French knots.

You will need

For a finished throw 35" (88cm) square:
1yd (90cm) heavy white linen fabric, 36" (90cm) wide
1yd (90cm) blue cotton or linen fabric, 36" (90cm) wide, for backing
1yd (90cm) calico, 36" (90cm) wide, for interlining
Assorted floral furnishing fabrics in various weights
8" x 12" (20 x 30cm) each red, blue, and lime-green cotton fabrics
8" (20cm) square emerald cotton fabric
Toning and contrasting pearl cottons
Matching and contrasting sewing threads

To prepare the appliqué

1 Sort through the furnishing fabrics, selecting the most interesting flower motifs in a range of sizes. Look for a variety of colors and shapes, making sure that some are complete with stems. Cut out about 20 assorted flowers, leaving a ¼" (6mm) seam allowance all around. Clip the curves and points, then fold the seam allowances to the wrong side and baste (fig 1).

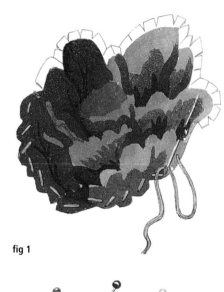

fig 1

fig 2

2 Cut out at least 10 different printed leaves from the remaining furnishing fabrics, leaving a ¼" (6mm) seam allowance around each. Enlarge the template shapes for the leaves on page 69 to 150% on a photocopier. Using these as a guide, cut out about 35 plain-colored leaves, in various sizes, from the 4 different-colored plain cotton fabrics, adding the seam allowance to each shape. Clip curves and points, then turn under and baste seam allowances.

3 Enlarge the chrysanthemum-shaped flower template on page 69 to 150%, and use as a guide to cut a flower from plain blue cotton fabric, leaving a ¼" (6mm) seam allowance all around the shape. Clip the curves and points, then turn under the seam allowances and baste them in place.

4 Extra definition can be given to some of the motifs by mounting them on plain-colored flower shapes. Select some cutout and edge-finished printed roses with strong outlines, and draw around them on the remaining red and green cotton fabric, using a chalk marking pencil. Cut out, leaving a margin of at least ¾" (2cm) all around. Clip the curves and points, turn under ¼" (6mm), and baste. Pin, then baste the printed flowers centrally on top of the plain ones (fig 2).

5 Enlarge the stylized butterfly template on page 69 to 150% as before, and use as a guide to cut one shape from suitably patterned furnishing fabric, leaving a ¼" (6mm) seam allowance all around.

To assemble the design

1 Press the white linen background fabric, and check that the edges are square. Lay the fabric flat on your work surface, and begin by placing the largest flowers in position. Create a visual focus by concentrating the motifs near one corner, then scattering the rest across the square.

2 Place the prepared leaves and butterfly between the flowers, overlapping some of the motifs and leaving space around others. Vary the density of the groupings to give balance to the design, and take time to move the various motifs around until you are happy with the overall arrangement. Pin, then baste the motifs in their final positions.

fig 3

fig 4

fig 5

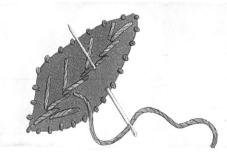

To embroider the motifs

1 Sew each flower in place, using a contrasting or toning pearl cotton. Use overcast stitch or blanket stitch around the outer edges, then add further decoration with a selection of stitches in the same or another color. Use French knots, stem stitch, satin stitch, and straight stitch to highlight details, such as petal outlines or the centers of the flowers. Vary the design by embroidering stamens from some of the flowers to extend onto the backing fabric, using straight stitch and French knots (fig 3).

2 Sew the butterfly in place with an invisible slipstich, using matching sewing thread. Embroider the details, using pearl cotton in colors to tone with the printed fabric. Then work the body and wing markings in satin stitch. Add more details to the wings with French knots, circled by running stitch. Indicate the antennae with straight lines of running stitch, finished off with French knots (fig 4).

3 Stitch the printed leaves in place in the same way as for the flowers, picking out

some of the printed lines with embroidery. Stitch the plain leaves in place, using matching or contrasting pearl cotton threads, and indicate the veins with feather, straight, stem, or running stitches (fig 5).

4 Remove all the basting threads, and press the appliqué on the right side, using a pressing cloth.

To finish the throw

1 Press the blue cotton or linen backing fabric and the calico interlining. Place the appliqué right side up on your work surface. Position the interlining and then the backing fabric on top, lining up all the edges. Pin through all 3 layers.

2 Machine stitch around all 4 sides with a seam allowance of ½" (12mm), leaving a 10" (25cm) gap at one side. Remove the pins, and trim the corners.

3 Turn the throw right side out through the gap, and slipstitch the open sides together by hand. Press lightly on the reverse (blue) side.

4 Finish off by working a line of French knots ¼" (6mm) from the edge, using blue pearl cotton. Sew through the top layer of fabric only, working the stitches approximately ½" (12mm) apart.

Enlarge the motifs to 150% on a photocopier, and use as templates for the appliqué. Add a ¼" (6mm) seam allowance when cutting out the fabric.

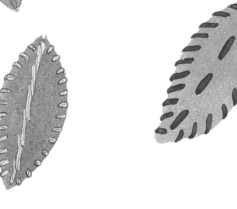

sporting pillows

These eclectic pillows use the new technique of image transfer, but would not have looked out of place in the study of an Edwardian country gentleman. Old black-and-white prints of sporting pursuits acquired from an antiquarian bookseller have been applied to cream cloth and combined with a mixture of fabrics – bright and muted tweeds, tartans, and woven stripes. The final, innovative touch comes from the accessories: blazer buttons, braids, and golf tees.

Golf pillow

You will need

For a pillow 14" (35cm) square:

15" (38cm) square dark tartan fabric, for pillow front

15" (38cm) square matching tartan fabric, for pillow back

Brightly colored tweed and tartan woolen fabric scraps

5" x 6¾" (13 x 17cm) cream cotton fabric

Black sewing thread

Tweed- or textured sport-weight knitting yarn

12 wooden golf tees in assorted colors

Drill with fine bit

4 buttons, with golfing logo if possible

Illustration of golfer

Cream paper

Image transfer fluid

Pillow form to fit cover

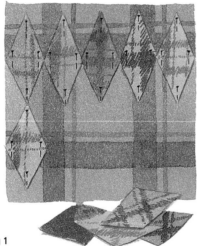

fig 1

To make the pillow front

1 Make a diamond template to the dimensions given on page 71, and cut out. Use the template as a guide to cut out 10 diamonds from brightly colored tweed and tartan fabric scraps. Cut them so that they lie along the grain of the fabric, with stripes running from top to bottom. Pin and baste the diamonds in 2 rows of 5 to the square of dark tartan fabric (fig 1).

2 Set your sewing machine to a wide zigzag, and stitch around the edges of the diamond shapes so that the raw edges are covered.

3 Lay lengths of tweed- or textured

knitting yarn across the diamonds to form an argyle pattern. The yarn should be parallel to the edges of the diamonds and cross in the center of each shape. Pin, then stitch in place with a wide machine zigzag worked right over the yarn to hold it down (fig 2). Press the pillow front.

4 Photocopy the golfing image that you have selected onto cream paper, enlarging or reducing it as necessary so that it fits on the cream cotton fabric. Following the manufacturer's

70   fig 2

Enlarge this diamond template to 6¼" (158mm) high by 3" (77mm) wide.

instructions, use image transfer fluid to transfer the picture centrally onto the cream fabric.

5 Place the golfer on the left-hand side of the pillow front, and pin around the outside edge. Border the image with a double length of knitting yarn, then stitch in place with a wide zigzag.

To finish the pillow

1 With right sides together, pin the pillow back to the matching tartan fabric for the front. Sew around 3 sides with a seam allowance of ½" (12mm), leaving the bottom edge open. Trim the corners, and turn the cover right side out. Use the point of your embroidery scissors to ease the corners into shape, and insert the pillow form. Slipstitch the fourth side together. Sew a button to each corner of the pillow front.

2 To finish, use a drill with a fine bit to make a small hole ⅜" (8mm) from the end of each of the golfing tees, and sew 3 tees loosely to each point of the pillow to form a "tassel."

Cricket pillow

fig 1

fig 2

You will need

For a pillow 13" x 17" (33 x 44cm):
14" x 18" (35 x 45cm) cream cotton fabric, for pillow front
14" x 18" (35 x 45cm) sea-green moiré, for pillow back
4 differently patterned striped ties
60" (1.5m) striped braid, 1" (2.5cm) wide
40" (1m) striped braid, ½" (1.5cm) wide
Matching sewing threads
4 gold blazer buttons
Illustration of cricket player
Cream paper
Image transfer fluid (available from good notions departments and art shops)
Pillow form to fit cover

To make the pillow front

1 Photocopy your image onto cream paper, enlarging or reducing it to fit within a rectangle measuring 6¼" x 7½" (16 x 19cm). Use image transfer fluid to transfer the image onto the cream cotton fabric, as indictated in the manufacturer's instructions.

2 Cut 2 8" (20cm) lengths from each of the striped braids. Pin, then sew a narrow strip and a wide strip on each side of the image.

3 Arrange the 4 ties to form a frame around the center panel. The wide points should all overlap in the same direction. Pin them in place, and trim off the ends (fig 1). Machine stitch them in place with straight stitch, keeping the needle close to the edges of the striped fabric.

To make the corner tabs

The 4 corners are all trimmed in the same way. For each, cut 2 5" (12cm) lengths from wide braid and one from narrow braid. Fold the lengths in half, and pin to the right side of the corner so that the 2 wider loops lie along the corners and the narrower loop points toward the center of the pillow. Baste in place around the outer edge (fig 2).

To finish the pillow

1 With right sides together, pin the pillow back to the front. Sew around 3 sides with a seam allowance of ½" (12mm), leaving the bottom edge open. Trim the corners, and turn the cover right side out. With your embroidery scissors, ease the corners into shape, and insert the pillow form. Slipstitch the fourth side together.

2 Finish off by sewing a gold button to each corner of the pillow front.

Fishing pillow

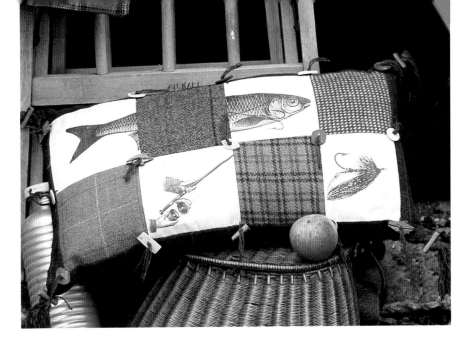

fig 1

fig 2

You will need

For a pillow 13" x 23" (33 x 58cm):
21½" x 30" (55 x 76cm) brown tweed
  fabric
4 6" (15cm) squares varied tweed fabrics
12" (30cm) square cream cotton fabric
15 wooden or coconut-shell buttons
Matching sewing threads
4 wooden toggle buttons
Tweed-effect brown fingering-weight
  knitting yarn
Illustrations of angling subjects
Cream paper
Image transfer fluid
Pillow form to fit cover

To make the pillow front

1 Photocopy the angling images you
have selected onto cream paper,
reducing or enlarging so that each will fit
within a 6" (15cm) square. Cut the
cream fabric into 4 6" (15cm) squares.
Using image transfer fluid and following
the manufacturer's instructions, transfer
one picture onto each square. A long
shape, such as a fish, can be divided so
that it appears across 2 of the squares.
2 Alternate the 4 tweed and 4 picture
squares to make a checkerboard
rectangle of 2 by 4. Stitch them together
in 2 strips of 4, leaving a seam allowance
of ½" (12mm) (fig 1). Join the strips

lengthwise, matching the seams. Press
the seams open: this must be done on
the back with a pressing cloth so that
the heat does not damage the images.
3 Cut a rectangle of brown tweed fabric
14" x 24" (36 x 61cm) for the pillow
back. From the remaining fabric, cut 2
strips 2½" x 24" (6.5 x 61cm) and 2
strips 2½" x 11" (6.5 x 28cm) to form a
border for the patchwork panel. Sew the
2 short lengths along the short ends of
the panel, then sew the 2 long lengths
along the long sides. Press the seams.
4 Use double lengths of tweed-effect
yarn to stitch the buttons in place at the
corners of each square. Knot the ends
and trim to 2½" (6cm) to form a tuft.

To finish the pillow

1 With right sides together, pin the
pillow back to the front around one
short and 2 long sides. Stitch, leaving a
seam allowance of ½" (12mm). Trim the
corners, and turn right side out. With the
point of your embroidery scissors, ease
the corners into shape, and insert the
pillow form. Slipstitch the fourth side.
2 To make a tassel for trimming each
corner, thread several strands of tweed-
effect yarn through the holes in a toggle
button. Tie in a knot, and trim to 2½"
(6cm). Sew firmly in place (fig 2).

73

floral tablecloth

Printed and woven fabrics are often used in a highly extravagant fashion, combining every variation of texture, pattern, and color. This unmistakably contemporary tablecloth demonstrates how a much simpler approach can be equally dramatic, bringing appliqué right up to date for a modern interior.

The success of such a minimalist treatment depends on a refined balance of form and stitch, along with the careful selection of fabrics. The vitality of the yellow and white linen background of the tablecloth is balanced by the precise placing of the stylized appliqué and embroidered flowers.

You will need

For a finished tablecloth about 58"
   (147cm) square:
⅞ yd (80cm) white linen fabric, 60"
   (150cm) wide
30" (76cm) square yellow linen fabric
30" (76cm) square yellow-and-white
   check cotton fabric
12" x 20" (30 x 50cm) cotton fabric in 2
   shades of green
Scraps of plain, check, and floral fabrics,
   including woven numbers and sprig
   prints
Matching and contrasting sewing threads
Assorted embroidery threads

To make the tablecloth

1 Cut the white linen fabric into 2 30" (76cm) squares. Pin, then machine stitch one of the pieces along one edge of the square of yellow linen fabric, with an allowance of ½" (12mm). Press the seam open. Fold under the raw edges along each side of the seam, and press flat. Machine stitch in place, using matching sewing thread (fig 1). Join the second square of white linen to the square of yellow-and-white check cotton fabric in the same way.

2 Join the 2 rectangles together, so that the white squares are diagonally opposite. Finish the seam as before, then finish the outside edge with a machine-stitched narrow double hem, using a contrasting thread.

To prepare and assemble the appliqué

1 Cut 12 tapering strips from the 2 shades of green cotton fabric. These should vary in size, ¾"–1½" (2–4cm) wide and 9"–18" (23–45cm) long. Finish the raw edges by pressing under an allowance of ¼" (6mm) all around.

2 Place the strips on the tablecloth, adjusting their positions as desired to give a balanced overall composition. When you are satisfied with the arrangement, pin, then machine stitch the strips in place, using matching green sewing threads.

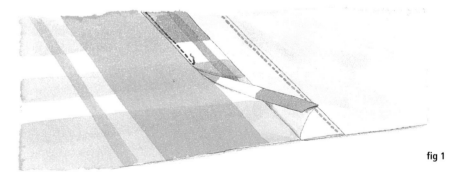

fig 1

fig 2

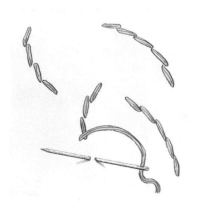

fig 3

3 Trace the various templates shown below. Using these as a guide and adding a seam allowance of ¼" (6mm) all around, cut out a selection of leaf and flower shapes from both plain and patterned fabrics. Choose predominately green fabrics for the leaves, and both flowered and colored fabrics for the petals – look for interesting pattern areas or pick out single floral motifs of a suitable size.

4 Clip the curves of the motifs, and press under the edges. Take some time in arranging the motifs on the tablecloth until you are happy with the overall design, then pin them to the tablecloth, and machine stitch in place using matching sewing threads.

To embroider the motifs and background
1 Add contrasting colored detail to the flowers and stems, either by hand with lines of running or straight stitch using embroidery thread (fig 2), or by machine with the controls set to the longest straight stitch. Using bright red thread, stitch tulip-shaped petals at the top of one of the stems, filling them with lines of backstitch or straight machine stitching. Using contrasting colors of sewing thread, work long lines of machine straight stitch across the width of the tablecloth.

2 Hand embroider decorative circles and random patterns of backstitch, running stitch, stem stitch, and French knots across the tablecloth (fig 3).

These templates are shown actual size. Add a ¼" (6mm) seam allowance all around when cutting out the fabric.

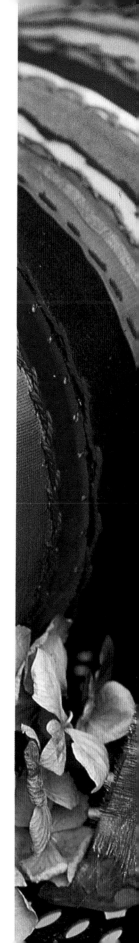

Lace, ribbons, & organza

Lace has always been the ultimate luxury fabric. Handmade lace cuffs and collars were once worn as status symbols by both men and women of fashion, and – along with woven braids, cords, and ribbons – lace has long been favored by dressmakers to add the final touch to a special outfit. Well-chosen trimmings can also give a decorative, opulent finish to other needlecrafts, particularly appliqué.

Trimmings can be sewn to functional fabrics, such as unbleached calico, for a striking effect, or used together with net, organza, or voile for more ethereal results. Ribbon or braid may be used to border a design, conceal a seam, or even to create a fabric made up entirely of appliquéd bands of complementary colors and textures. With imagination, purely ornamental fabrics and trimmings can be combined to create stunning effects.

using trimmings

Most people who enjoy sewing gather a ragbag over time. Among the remnants of different fabrics there may be scraps of more luxurious materials such as velvets and organzas. There is also likely to be an accumulation of various trimmings – ribbons, braids, cords, and fringes, as well as scraps of lace – and all these can be incorporated into your appliqué projects. The Cactus Pillows shown on pages 88–93 are a wonderful example of how this can be done.

Ribbon

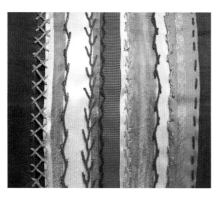

Ribbons have been used for many years both to hold together and to adorn garments and furnishing accessories. Decorative ribbon can be purchased in a wide variety of widths, textures, and colors, ranging from translucent voiles, ribbed grosgrain, and tartans, to printed striped, spotted, or patterned satins.

• Ribbon can be used with restraint in an appliqué design to provide a contrasting strip of color, or several ribbons can be interwoven to give an interesting multicolored effect.

• Lavish ribbons can be gathered into rosettes or tied into bows as extra embellishment to trim an item.

• The woven edges make ribbon simple to sew in place with hand stitching or by machine, as there are no raw edges to turn under. However, the stitching on both edges must always run in the same direction, for example, from top to bottom, to prevent the ribbon from becoming puckered and distorted.

Organza

Organza is a translucent fabric woven from silk, acetate, or metallic threads and is usually chosen by dressmakers to create extravagant ball gowns and evening dresses, or by milliners for adorning hats. On a smaller scale, it can be used very successfully for appliqué, both as a delicate background fabric and for lustrous motifs.

• Organza can be sewn onto or inserted into opaque fabrics, but it is most effective when layered with net, voile, or other sheer materials to exploit the play of light on the surface of the fabric. The Herb Bags on pages 82–85 show how subtle and unexpected color effects can be achieved in this way.

• Shot organza is woven from a contrasting warp and weft, which gives it an iridescent appearance. It is possible to utilize this quality by cutting out square or rectangular shapes along the grain of the fabric and fringing the raw edges to show the different-colored silk, gold, or silver threads.

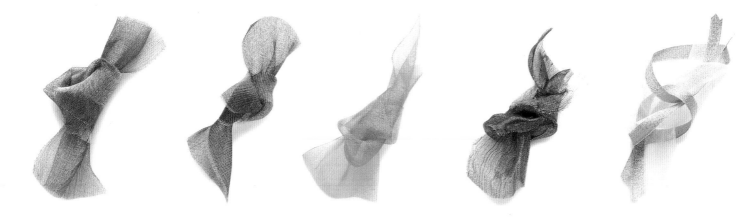

Lace　Modern machine lace is available in many decorative forms. Edgings are produced in various widths and weights, and lace is also manufactured in fabric widths for dressmaking. Lace usually only comes in white, but it can be dyed to any color for a more unconventional look. An antique beige tint can be given to new cotton lace by dipping it in cold tea or coffee.

Net-based laces, which are derived from traditional bobbin or needlepoint lace patterns, are often too fine to be used for any work that will need to withstand much wear, but thicker *guipure* lace, with its well-defined patterns, is ideal for appliqué. It can be used in two different ways – either inset into a background or applied on top of another fabric.

Applied lace

Choose a lace with a strong design, and cut out individual motifs, using sharp embroidery scissors. Some types of lace will not fray, but in order to prevent any unraveling it may be necessary to coat the back of the lace with a fray-prevention liquid (see page 24). This will give the lace a slightly stiffer texture that is easier to handle.

• Arrange the motifs on the background fabric, and pin in place. Large motifs should be basted in place to prevent any wrinkles. Then sew the motifs in place with neat overcast stitches (whipstitches) around the outside edges, using matching thread.

• Be careful not to pull the thread too tightly, especially when using a lightweight background fabric. A densely woven background, such as cotton or linen, will create a very different effect than a net or other sheer fabric.

Lace insertion

When lace is inset into a background, it becomes part of the fabric itself. If the lace is to be attached to a fine cloth, or you are working by hand on a small scale, the main fabric should be supported in an embroidery frame. For larger-scale work on heavier fabric, use a sewing machine to stitch the lace in position and to finish the raw edges with satin stitch.

• To insert by hand, cut out a single lace motif. Pin, then baste the motif to the background fabric. Stitch neatly in place with blanket or overcast stitch around the outside edges of the motif, using matching thread (fig 1).

Turn over, and carefully cut away the fabric from within the shape (fig 2) – nail scissors with small curved blades are ideal for this.

• To insert by machine, draw a shape onto a piece of lace using a dressmaker's pen, or cut out a motif, leaving a margin of ¼" (6mm) around the edge. Pin the lace to the background, then baste it carefully in place.

Stitch over the drawn outline, then trim away the surplus lace from the front, and the background fabric from behind, as above. Work a line of closely spaced satin machine stitch to conceal and strengthen the raw edges.

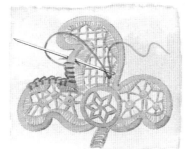

fig 1

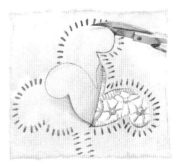

fig 2

herb bags

The translucent qualities of metallic organzas are exploited to the full to make these opulent herb bags. The sumptuous texture of the crushed velvet hearts contrasts with the delicacy of the sheer silk organzas, and the multilayered fabrics create a rich density of color. Lustrous beads, gold cords, and tassels are added as luxurious finishing touches.

The bags are very simple to put together and can be made in any size or combination of colors. They can be filled with dried flowers or herbs, as here, so that the colors of the leaves and petals show through the sheer fabrics, or be used as presentation bags for a special Christmas or birthday gift.

Rose bag

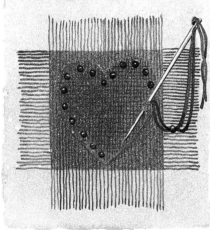

fig 1

You will need

14" x 18" (36 x 45cm) pale gold crystal organza
6¼" x 18" (16 x 45cm) silver crystal organza
Scraps of purple, pink, and turquoise shot-silk organzas
Scraps of gold and bronze metallic organzas
Matching sewing threads
Approximately 200 tiny metallic beads in various bright colors
Fine crewel (embroidery) needle (size 10)
Rose potpourri to fill

To work the appliqué and beading

1 Cut out 9 1½" (4cm) squares from the different shot-silk organzas, and fringe the edges by carefully pulling out a few threads along each side. Cut out a 5" (12cm) square of silver crystal organza, and fringe the edges. Arrange the small squares on it in 3 rows of 3, alternating the colors.

2 Using the 3 smallest templates shown below as a guide, cut out 9 different-sized hearts from metallic organzas, and pin each one to a contrasting square.

3 The appliqué is held on by the beading. Using a double length of matching sewing thread and the fine needle, stitch the metallic beads ⅛" (3mm) inside the edge of the hearts (fig 1).

To finish the bag

1 Hand sew the appliquéd panel to the center front of the pale gold crystal organza rectangle 1½" (4cm) from the lower short edge, using matching thread. With the appliqué on the inside, join the side edges by hand or machine. Fold the bag in half so that the seam runs up the center back, and join the bottom seam. Turn right side out.

2 Fold under the top 6" (15cm) of the bag fabric, and run a gathering stitch through both layers 3½" (9cm) from the top. Fill the bag with rose potpourri and pull the gathering thread.

3 Cut out a 18" x 1½" (45 x 4cm) strip of organza, and tie it around the top, with the bow facing toward the back.

These assorted heart motifs for the three herb bags on pages 82–85 are shown actual size.

Gold bag

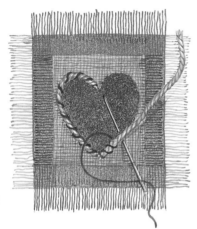

fig 1

You will need

10" x 12" (25 x 30cm) bronze Fortuny-pleat metallic fabric
Scrap of red velvet
Scraps of bronze and red shot metallic organzas
30" (75cm) gold cord
Matching sewing thread
Gold machine embroidery threads
Small piece of cardboard
Dried herbs to fill

To work the appliqué

1 Using the largest template shown on page 82 as a guide, cut out a heart from red velvet. Cut out a rectangle 3½" x 4" (9 x 10cm) from red shot metallic organza and a 2½" x 3" (6 x 7cm) rectangle from bronze. Fringe the edges of both by carefully pulling out a few threads along each side. Place the smaller rectangle on top of the larger, then pin the velvet heart in the center.
2 Sew the heart through both pieces of organza with small invisible overcast stitches, leaving a small space at the center top. Slip one end of the gold cord under the velvet at this point, then couch it around the edge of the heart, using matching sewing thread (fig 1). Trim the end of the cord to ¼" (6mm), tuck it under the velvet, and secure the raw edge with overcast stitches.

To finish the bag

1 Sew the appliquéd panel to the center front of the Fortuny-pleat metallic fabric 2" (5cm) from the lower long edge. With the appliqué on the inside, join the two short edges by hand or machine, then fold in half so that the center seam runs up the back, and join lower edge.
2 Unravel a few long threads from the top edge to make a narrow fringe. Turn right side out.
3 Make 2 tassels about 3½" (9cm) long, using gold machine embroidery thread. Knot the ends of the remaining length of gold cord, and sew a tassel to each end to conceal cut cord ends.
4 Fill the bag with dried herbs, then tie the cord in a bow around the top.

Lavender bag

You will need

17" x 18" (43 x 45cm) silver crystal organza
2½" x 5½" (6 x 14cm) gold metallic organza
Scraps of emerald and lilac velvet
Scraps of metallic organza in golds, greens, and blues
Matching sewing threads
Approximately 180 translucent ⅛" (3mm) glass beads
Fine crewel (embroidery) needle (size 10)
24" (60cm) gold cord
Dried lavender to fill

To work the appliqué

1 Trace the 4 heart templates shown on page 82 onto paper. Selecting from these, draw 3 hearts onto the reverse of each of the emerald and lilac velvet fabrics, and cut out.
2 Cut out a rectangle 2½" x 5½" (6 x 14cm) from gold metallic organza, and a rectangle 2" x 5" (5 x 13cm) from silver crystal organza. Cut out 3 1½" (4cm) squares and 3 1¼" (3cm) squares from the various scraps of organza. Fringe the edges of all the pieces by carefully pulling out a few threads along each side.
3 Place the smaller organza rectangle on top of the larger one, then arrange the 3 larger organza squares in a row. Set the smaller squares on them at an angle, then pin a velvet heart onto each square. Sew the hearts in place with small overcast stitches, using matching sewing threads. Make sure that you stitch through all the layers of organza.
4 Cut out a rectangle 15" x 18" (38 x 45cm) from silver crystal organza to make the main bag, and fringe one of the short sides to form the lower edge. Then pin the appliquéd organza panel to the center front of the bag 2" (5cm) from the bottom.

To sew on the beads

1 The panel is held on by the beading. Using a double length of matching sewing thread and the fine needle, stitch translucent glass beads as close as possible to the edge of the velvet hearts, spacing them evenly.

2 Pin the remaining 3 hearts to the main bag, scattering them above the appliquéd panel. Sew them in place with tiny overcast stitches, using matching sewing thread, then edge with a line of beading as above.

To finish the bag

1 With the appliqué on the inside, join the side edges of the bag by hand or machine. Turn the bag right side out, and then fold so that the seam runs up the center back. Close the lower edge with a line of running stitch, using matching metallic sewing thread and the fine needle and threading on a few beads as you work (fig 1).

2 Make a knot at each end of the gold cord, and unravel the threads to create a tassel effect. Fold under the top 6" (15cm) of the bag fabric, and run a gathering stitch through both layers of fabric 3½" (9cm) from the top. Fill the bag with dried lavender, and pull the gathering thread. Secure the ends of the thread tightly, then finish off by tying the gold cord in a bow.

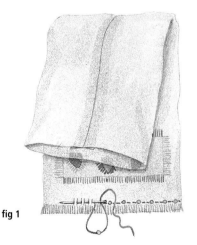

fig 1

ribbon bolster

The attractive striped pattern on this bolster pillow is formed by stitching bands of ribbon to a taffeta background. Its strong visual impact is achieved by using an assortment of fabric texture, but limiting the color scheme to a narrow range. Some ribbons are overlapped to give extra density to the color, while in other places parts of the tartan background show through. The embroidery stitches that hold the ribbons in place are reminiscent of those used to embellish Victorian "crazy patchwork".

You will need

For a bolster 20" (50cm) long:
43" (110cm) lengths of at least 15 ribbons in different widths, textures, and colors
21" x 25" (54 x 64cm) dark striped or tartan taffeta fabric, stripes running parallel to shorter edges
Toning and contrasting pearl cottons
Matching sewing threads
Strong thread, such as buttonhole thread, for gathering
20" (50cm) bolster pillow form, 20" (50cm) circumference
2 furnishing tassels (optional)

To work the appliqué

1 Cut the lengths of ribbon in half, and place them on the taffeta fabric so that they lie parallel to the shorter edges. Use the stripes of the fabric as a guide to keeping the ribbons straight, and leave ½" (12mm) uncovered at each short edge. Butt together the edges of most of the ribbons, but leave narrow gaps between others so that the taffeta shows. Overlap some of the plain colors with sheer ribbons. Adjust until there is a good balance of color and texture.

2 Pin the ribbons carefully in place, and baste along both edges. Work each line of basting in the same direction to prevent puckering (fig 1).

3 Secure the ribbons with lines of embroidery worked in contrasting or toning pearl cottons. Use simple stitches including herringbone, feather, running, and whipped running stitch, but vary the width, length, and spacing to give extra interest to the surface. When all the ribbons have been sewn in place, remove the basting.

To finish the bolster

1 With right sides facing, pin together the long edges of the appliquéd taffeta, insuring that the cut ends of the ribbons match. Machine stitch together, leaving a seam allowance of ½" (12mm), then turn the cover right side out.

2 Place the cover over the bolster: it should fit tightly. Turn under the taffeta at each short edge, and using a double length of strong thread, stitch with a line of evenly spaced running stitches about ½" (12mm) long. Pull this thread tightly so that the ends of the bolster are covered. Make sure that the gathers are evenly spaced, then finish off with a few overcast stitches to secure.

3 Conceal the gathered ends with a trimming such as tassels or ribbon bows.

fig 1

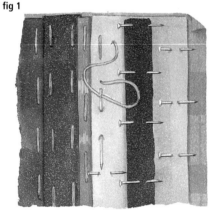

cactus pillows

An extravagant, unrestrained use of color within a carefully chosen palette characterizes these large and exuberant pillows. The cotton lace belies its delicate appearance and has been combined with unexpected fabrics, including terry cloth, over-dyed gingham, velvet, and organza. Furnishing braids, bullion and pompon fringe, beads, and ribbons in matching and clashing shades add texture and pattern to both the fronts and backs of the pillow covers. This project is open to a very individual interpretation. Search through your ragbag of remnants and scraps to find an assortment of interesting and unusual fabrics, and indulge in a vibrant riot of color.

Rectangular pillow

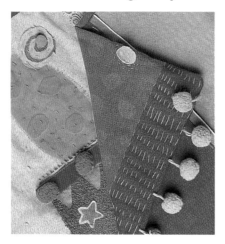

You will need

For a pillow 16" x 24" (40 x 60cm):
For the front panel and appliqué:
Remnants and scraps of fabric in
   assorted patterns, textures, and colors
Assorted thick cotton lace, pompon
   fringe, bullion fringe, cord, ribbon,
   and rickrack
Ribbon rose
Matching sewing thread
Contrasting pearl and soft embroidery
   cottons, and cotton embroidery floss
Fabric glue
For the back:
8" x 25" (20 x 63.5cm) cotton fabric
12½" x 25" (32 x 63.5cm) contrasting
   cotton fabric
25" (63.5cm) braid
Contrasting cotton embroidery floss
3 self-cover button molds, ¾" (20mm)
   diameter
25" (63.5cm) pompon fringe
Pillow form to fit cover

To make the front panel

1 Cut out 3 rectangles from contrasting bright cotton fabrics: 2 9½" x 14" (24 x 36cm) and one 8" x 14" (20 x 36cm). Join the rectangles together with a seam allowance of ½" (12mm) to make a larger rectangle measuring 14" x 25" (36 x 63.5cm). Then press the stitched seams open.
2 Cut out 2 25" (63.5cm) strips, each 2½" (6cm) wide, in a fourth color, and sew to each long side of the main fabric with a ½" (12mm) seam allowance. Then press the seams open. Decorate the strips with parallel lines of large running stitch, worked in a contrasting embroidery thread.

To work the appliqué

1 Enlarge the 3 outlines on page 92 to 156%, then to 125% on a photocopier. Trace the main elements of each template. Using these as a guide, cut out the cacti and their pots from an assortment of fabrics. Arrange the pieces on the background following fig 1 and the photograph opposite. Stick in place, using fabric glue.
2 Cut out the stars, circles, and stripes that trim the pots, and the small dots and circles that decorate the cacti, and glue in place. Add further embellishment to the appliqué with pompons cut from lengths of fringe, ribbons, bullion fringe and lace, rickrack and a ribbon rose.
3 Embroider the details, using a variety of embroidery threads in bright colors: straight stitch for the spikes around the edges of the cacti, running-stitch lines to hold down the rickrack, and couching to secure colored cord.

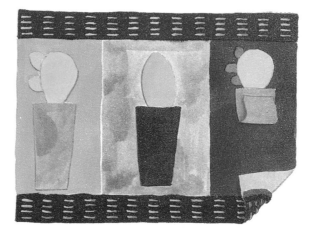

fig 1

fig 2

fig 3

fig 4

fig 5

To make the pillow back

1 Cut out 2 rectangles, one 8" x 25" (20 x 63.5cm) and one 12½" x 25" (32 x 63.5cm) from contrasting cotton fabrics. Also cut out a 25" (63.5cm) strip, 2½" (6cm) wide, from fabric to match the narrower piece.

2 Finish one long raw edge of the larger rectangle. Turn under a 2" (5cm) hem.

3 Trim one long edge of the narrower rectangle with braid, by stitching it between the main fabric and the strip, with the right side of the braid facing the right side of the main fabric (fig 2). Turn back the fabric and press. Topstitch with a line of running stitch, using embroidery floss in a bright color (fig 3).

4 Make 3 evenly spaced buttonholes on the braid-trimmed piece. For each one, cut out a 1½" (4cm) square of contrasting fabric, and draw an opening 1" x ¼" (2.5cm x 5mm) on the center. Baste the square to the right side of the fabric, and sew around the outline by hand or machine. Slit the fabric inside the stitching, cutting carefully into the corners (fig 4), and push the remaining fabric to the wrong side. Press, then topstitch the opening with embroidery floss in a bright color (fig 5). Finish the raw edges of the fabric at the back.

To finish the pillow

1 Pin pompon fringe along the bottom edge of the appliquéd front, with the pompons facing inward. With right sides together, pin the trimmed back piece along this edge, then pin the second back piece in place so that it overlaps. Sew all around the outside, with a seam allowance of ½" (12mm). Turn the cover right side out.

2 Following the manufacturer's instructions, cover 3 self-cover button molds with different-colored fabrics, and sew in place on the back of the pillow. Insert the pillow form in the cover, and fasten the buttons.

Square pillow

You will need

For a pillow 24" (60cm) square:
For the front panel and appliqué:
Remnants and scraps of fabric in assorted patterns, textures, and colors
3 12" x 15" (30 x 38cm) pieces different-colored cotton fabrics, for the scallops
Assorted cords, ribbons, pompons, fringe, beads, rickrack, and felt
Matching sewing thread
Contrasting colors of pearl and soft embroidery cottons, and cotton embroidery floss
Fabric glue
For the back:
18" x 25" (45 x 63.5cm) cotton fabric
5" x 25" (13 x 63.5cm) matching cotton fabric
12" x 25" (30 x 63.5cm) contrasting cotton fabric
Self-cover button molds:
    3 1¼" (3cm) diameter
    2 ¾" (2cm) diameter
Felt scraps
Beads and/or embroidery threads as above
5 clear snaps
Pillow form to fit cover

To join the front cover

Cut out 3 rectangles from contrasting cotton fabrics, one 11" x 25" (28cm x 63.5cm), one 14½" x 15½" (37 x 39cm) and one 10½" x 14½" (27 x 37cm). Join them together to make a 25" (63.5cm) square, using fabric glue and simple running and overcast stitches.

fig 1

To work the appliqué

1 Enlarge the templates on pages 92 and 93 to 156%, then to 125% on a photocopier. Trace a separate pattern for each element. Cut out the main cactus parts and the flowerpots. Using fig 1 and the photograph on page 89 as a guide, glue them to the background.

2 Cut out the various stars that surround the smaller cactus, and the stars and circles that decorate the larger one and its pot, and glue them in place (fig 1). Sew beads, pompons, and lengths of ribbon and rickrack onto and around the pots and cacti. Embroider lines of running and straight stitch to highlight the motifs and to indicate the cactus spikes, using a variety of threads.

To make the scallops

Enlarge the scallop template on page 93 to 156%, then to 125% on a photocopier. You will need 16 scallops in assorted colors. For each scallop, cut 2 pieces of matching fabric, using the template as a guide. With right sides facing, stitch them together around the curved side with a seam allowance of ¼" (6mm). Clip the curves so that the seam will lie flat, turn right side out, and press the scallops flat.

To prepare the pillow back

1 Finish one long raw edge on the narrow strip of cotton fabric for the pillow back. To make a wavy edge on the larger rectangle for the pillow back, pin the narrow strip along one edge with right sides and raw edges together.

2 On the strip, draw a regular wavy line with 5 equidistant points ¼" (6mm) from

the raw edge (fig 2), and machine stitch along the line. Trim the 2 layers of fabric ¼" (6mm) outside the wavy line. Clip the seam allowance, and turn the fabric right side out. Press the wavy edges, then topstitch with a line of large-scale running stitch, using a contrasting embroidery thread. Finish one long raw edge on the other back piece.

To make the pillow

1 Lay the appliquéd piece right side up. Arrange 4 scallops pointing inward along each of the 4 edges.

2 Place the wavy-edged backing piece face down on the appliquéd square, matching raw edges along the bottom and with the wavy edge toward the center. Place the other backing piece face down along the other side, with the finished edge toward the center. Pin down, then sew around all 4 sides ½" (12mm) from the edge. Turn the pillow cover right side out.

To finish the pillow

1 To make the floral buttons, cover the 5 button molds with different-colored fabrics, following the manufacturer's instructions. Enlarge the flower template on page 93 to 156%, then to 125% on a photocopier. Using the template as a guide, cut out 5 flower shapes from felt. Snip a tiny hole in the center of each, and fit it over the shank before attaching the back piece (fig 3). Embellish each button with French knots or beads.

2 Sew one button to each point of the wavy edge. Sew a clear snap under the tip of each point, lining up the 2 parts carefully on both sides of the cover.

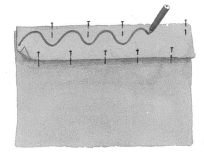

fig 2

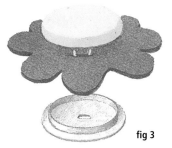

fig 3

cactus template for rectangular pillow

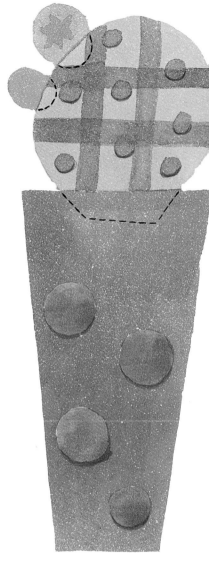

Enlarge all the motifs to 156% and then to 125% on the photocopier, and use as templates for the appliqué.

star template for square pillow

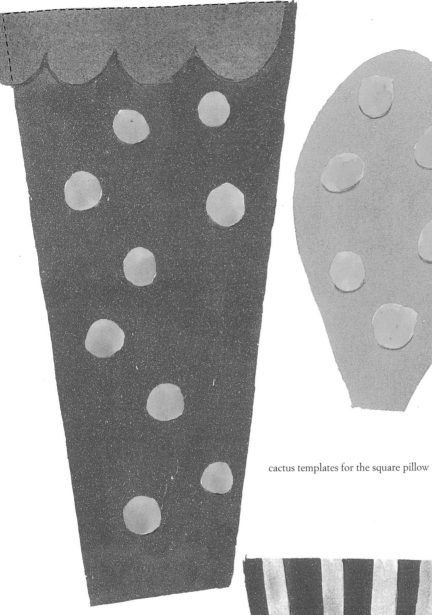

template for the
floral buttons on
the square pillow

cactus templates for the square pillow

scallop template for square pillow

93

lace blind

The formal lines of this classic roller blind are softened by the light filtering through the appliquéd lace cutouts. The blind provides a dramatic focus to a room, and the muted tones of unbleached calico and cotton lace will blend with any color scheme – old lace may be too fragile to withstand everyday use, but new lace can be dipped in tea to give it an antique appearance. The main central motif contains an initial to add a personal touch, but this can be replaced by a house or apartment number if the blind is to hang at a front window. An alphabet and a set of numerals are given on pages 106 and 107.

Blind kits, containing all the necessary accessories and instructions, are widely available in standard sizes that can be adapted easily to fit your own window. Finish off the lower edge of the blind with a wooden blind pull or a cream tassel.

You will need

Heavyweight unbleached calico, 4" (10cm) wider and 12" (30cm) longer than your window
25" (63cm) cotton lace, 5" (12cm) wide, or scraps of old lace and doilies
6" x 12" (15 x 30cm) cotton net, for main central motif
5" (12cm) square unbleached calico, for initial or number
Cream sewing thread
Window blind kit and spray-on fabric stiffener
Adhesive tape

To transfer the design

1 Enlarge the template on page 96 to 156%, and then 112% on a photocopier. Make a second copy. Reverse one section of the design, and join the 2 halves to make a symmetrical stencil. Cut out the various shapes.
2 Fold the unbleached calico for the blind in half lengthwise, and press lightly to mark the center line. Pin the stencil along this line so that it lies 6" (15cm) from the bottom edge. Using the stencil as a guide, mark the design on the fabric, using a dressmaker's pen (fig 1).

To work the appliqué

1 Cut lengths of lace to fit over the various small outlined sections of the design, allowing a minimum overlap of ½" (12mm) all around. Pin, then baste them in place ¼" (6mm) outside the outline of each shape, making sure that the lace lies flat (fig 2). If the outline has become indistinct, draw over it again on the lace. Using cream sewing thread, work straight machine stitch over the outline, stitching slowly to achieve smooth curves.
2 Trim the surplus lace to within ⅛" (3mm) of the stitched line, using sharp embroidery scissors (fig 3). Turn over the fabric, and carefully cut out the calico from within the shapes, to within ⅛" (3mm) of the stitching. Sew over the raw edges with a wide, medium-spaced zigzag stitch to finish and strengthen the seams (see photograph on page 96).

fig 1

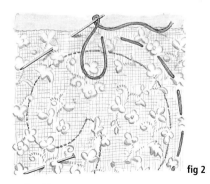

fig 2

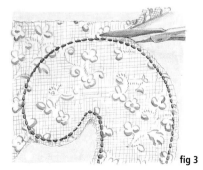

fig 3

3 Inset cotton net into the main central motif in the same way. Decorate the central motif either with small shapes cut from lace scraps, or with an appliquéd number or letter cut from unbleached calico. Baste, then hand sew or zigzag stitch in place.

4 Press well to remove the creases, using a pressing cloth to protect the lace.

To finish the blind

Check that the edges of the calico are square; trim them if not, then spray with fabric stiffener. Follow the instructions supplied with the kit to make up the blind. Screw the brackets to the wall as instructed, and fix the roller in place.

Half the design for the Lace Blind is shown here. Enlarge to 156% and then to 112% on a photocopier. Repeat to make a second copy. Reverse one half and join to the other along the center line to make a symmetrical shape.

center line

Patterns & motifs

The following pages offer a range of additional design motifs that will complement the projects in the earlier chapters and provide inspiration for you to develop further your own ideas. They include templates for four more country-style floral patterns, variations on the natural imagery of leaves and snowflakes, more distinctive nursery appliqué shapes for children, and finally two versatile alphabets that can be used on any scale to personalize your work.

block motifs

See Baltimore Bride Pillow on page 20

These blocks are inspired by antique originals but have been adapted to incorporate the distinctive floral motif from the Baltimore Bride Pillow. Like the rose-filled basket, the cornucopia is a symbol of abundance, often used on wedding quilts, and this example overflows with fruits and flowers. A full-sized appliqué bedspread is a true labor of love, but these four traditional patterns could be used together to make a crib cover or wall hanging. To achieve smooth curves, the circle for the garland and the curved stalks should all be made from bias strips (see page 16). Enlarge or reduce the motifs on a photocopier as desired.

pattern-cut snowflakes

See Snowflake Pillows on page 32

A huge variety of symmetrical patterns can be cut from folded paper. These can then form the starting point for creating intricate pattern-cut appliqué designs. To make a square shape, fold the paper diagonally in half, then into quarters, then into eighths, and press the creases firmly in place. Trace one section of the motif onto the triangle of folded paper and cut out. For a six-sided motif, fold the paper in half. Mark angles of 60° and 120° from the center, and fold again along these lines to give six segments, then fold the paper again before transferring the snowflake outline onto the top layer. Enlarge or reduce the motifs on a photocopier as desired.

leaf collection

See Leaf Table Linen on page 42

The morning glory, ivy, and passion flower templates can be used singly or arranged to form sprays to match the other leaf designs. The beech and silver birch leaves illustrated here are both used on the bright cotton tablecloth, but all of these designs could be adapted to a more naturalistic color scheme of summer greens or browns, yellows, and russets. Try cutting out an assortment of leaves in different shapes and sizes and arranging them randomly so that they overlap to create a true autumnal feel. Enlarge the motifs to 136% on a photocopier.

ivy

beech

passion flower

silver birch

horse chestnut

morning glory

103

nursery motifs

See Alphabet Quilt on page 56

These motifs – which include winter mittens, a car, a shell and an ice cream – are intended as variations for the red-and-white alphabet play quilt, but could equally well decorate children's clothes, bed linen, toy bags, or playroom pillows and curtains. The original quilt is made up in a restrained two-color combination, but try using a range of brightly colored cottons or small-scale dress prints for a more lively effect. Enlarge or reduce the motifs on a photocopier as desired.

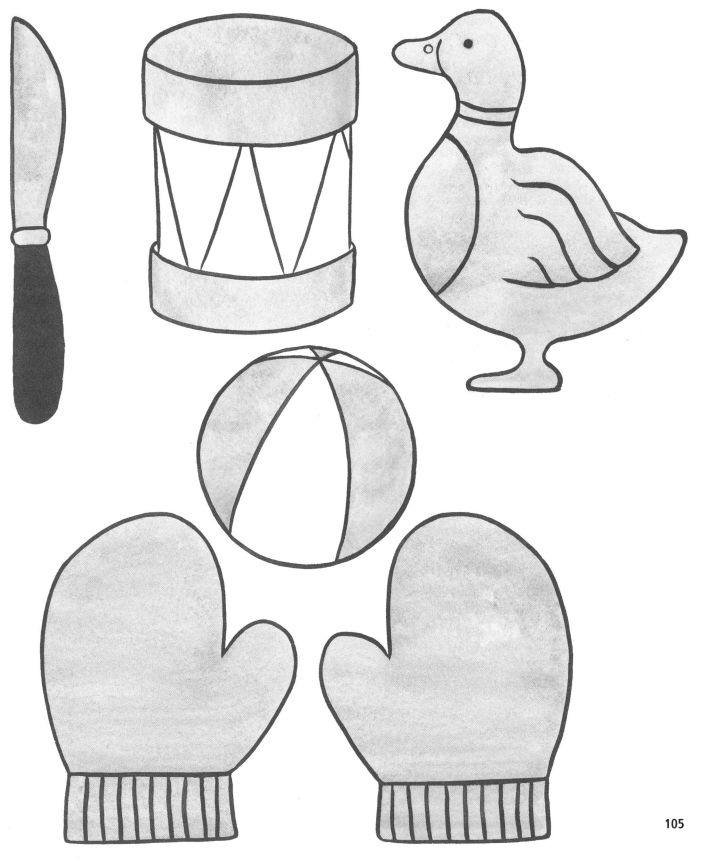

alphabets & numerals

Large or small single capital letters can be used to form monograms or sets of initials that add an individual finish to any appliqué project or gift, or you may choose them to build up words, names or short phrases. The plainer alphabet on pages 108 and 109 is used on the Alphabet Quilt on page 56, and the more ornate period variation shown here is intended for the Lace Blind on page 94, but either of them could be incorporated into other designs.

The two sets of numerals can also be adapted for many different purposes. To use as templates for the Lace Blind, enlarge the letters or numerals shown here to 156%, then 156%, then 140% on a photocopier.

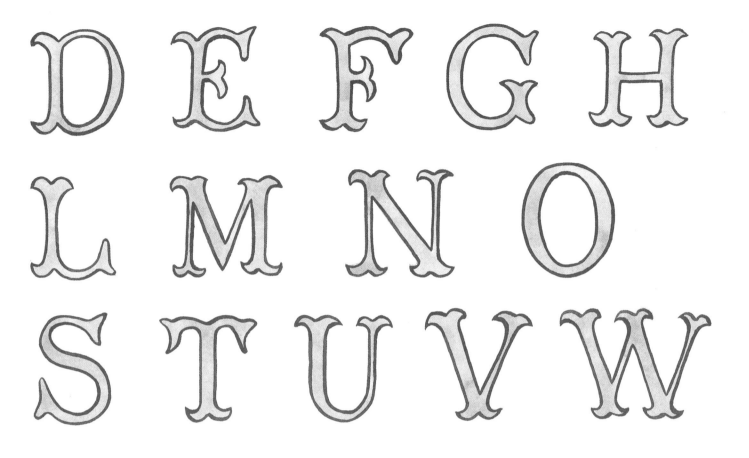

D E F G H
L M N O
S T U V W

6 7 8 9 0

FGHIJK
QRSTU

Enlarge the alphabets and numerals shown here to 156% and then to 106% on a photocopier and use as templates for the Alphabet Quilt on page 56.

ghijklm
uvwxyz
7890

109

index

acknowledgments

The author would like to thank everybody who has been involved in creating this book, particularly the editorial and design team at Quadrille who made it all possible: Mary Evans, Jane O'Shea, Patsy North, Vanessa Courtier, Kate Simunek for the illustrations, Pia Tryde for the photographs , and especially Gabi Tubbs for her inspiration.

Special thanks to Christine Kingdom at C. M. Offray & Son Ltd and Carole Tompkins for their help, and to my family for their unfailing support.

The author and publisher would also like to thank the textile artists who designed and made the following projects: Petra Boase (Cactus Pillows), Freddie Robins of Tait & Style (Animal Scarves and Sporting Pillows), Karen Spurgin (Broderie Perse Throw and Ribbon Bolster), Kelie-Marie Townsend (Kitchen Curtains), Lisa Vaughan (Floral Tablecloth) and Melanie Williams (Snowflake Pillows, Leaf Table Linen, and the Workbag, Housewife & Needlebook).
Denim flags, Hearts Edging, Alphabet Quilt, Lace Blind and Herb Bags were designed and made by the author.

Photographs on pages 36/7 and 43 by David George. China and glass (pages 36/7) and jug and glass (page 43) from The Conran Shop. The publisher thanks Jane Newdick for styling the photography, Ian Muggeridge for D.T.P. assistance, and Sally Harding for her invaluable editorial assistance.